TRADITIONAL
GARDEN DECOR

TRADITIONAL
GARDEN DECOR

Robin Langley Sommer

THUNDER BAY
P·R·E·S·S

Published in the United States by
Thunder Bay Press
An imprint of the Advantage Publishers Group
5880 Oberlin Drive, Suite 400
San Diego, CA 92121-4794
http://www.advantagebooksonline.com

Produced by
Saraband, The Arthouse, 752–756 Argyle Street,
Glasgow G3 8UJ, Scotland

ISBN 1-57145-551-5

10 9 8 7 6 5 4 3 2 1

Library of Congress Cataloging-in-Publication Data available upon request.

Page 1: An espaliered pear tree trained against the neat brickwork of this garden wall on the grounds of Leeds Castle, Kent, England. The county of Kent is known as "the Garden of England."

Page 2: A traditional birdbath makes an attractive focal point in this delightfully colorful cottage garden.

Page 3: A whimsical figure that recalls medieval gargoyles peeps out between tropical flowers and foliage.

Below: Trooper, a thirsty tabby cat, helps himself to refreshment.

THIS BOOK IS DEDICATED TO
TRISH LANGLEY, MAUREEN HUNT,
AND CYNTHIA PIKOR,
WITH LOVE FROM THEIR DAUGHTERS.

Contents

Introduction

The passion for creating gardens enhanced by the use of traditional ornament continues to grow, and never have there been so many beautiful objects and sources of inspiration available to the dedicated gardener. Books, magazines, catalogues, websites, television series, antique dealers, folk artists— all have contributed to the wealth of information and artefacts designed to complement every type of architecture and landscape. Local and national horticultural societies also enable gardeners to exchange ideas and experience, no matter the size of their properties and the formality or informality of their styles. Botanical gardens; arboretums; restored mansion/museums like Winterthur, created by Henry Francis du Pont in Delaware's scenic Brandywine Valley; and countless conservation and preservation groups nationwide have contributed to our growing awareness of traditional garden decor.

This type of cross-fertilization has far-reaching benefits for the community as well as the homeowner in terms of beautification, which is the antithesis of urban (and suburban) blight. Ugly chain-link fences and rigid concrete walkways are giving place to harmonious schemes in which fencing or hedging is in keeping with local

architecture, and inviting flagstone or gravel paths lead the eye through a garden gate toward an arbor wreathed in climbing vines, or an island bed defined by a Classical sundial. Here and there, we see encouraging signs that our long love affair with labor-intensive, chemically treated lawns is giving way to a spirit of adventure that favors the creation of "outdoor rooms" related by a cohesive plan. Larger perennial borders with four-season interest, informal "flowery meads" or meadows, water gardens, sheltered dining areas, pergolas, gazebos, fountains, and well-placed sculpture are regaining their rightful places in the domestic landscape.

Today one need not spend a queen's ransom on garden ornaments that contribute to a period ambience, whether Colonial, Victorian, Southwestern, or English-cottage style. There are treasures to be found at yard sales and flea markets, craft fairs and roadside antique shops. A weathered chair reclaimed from the attic or an old barn can serve as a resting place for a variety of colorful annuals in simple pots. New building materials like hypertufa (simulated stone) replicate the look of the timeworn stone troughs favored by English gardeners for centuries, and verdigris-finished brass provides weatherproof wind chimes, garden

Opposite: A scalloped stoneware birdbath surrounded by autumn flowers is enhanced by the "borrowed landscape" of the adjacent tall-grass prairie in Bureau County, Illinois.

Above: This handsome "ground basin" with Classical ornamentation was advertised by the British firm of Austin & Seeley in The Agricultural Gazette & Gardeners' Chronicle *for June 1857.*

stakes, and pedestal birdbaths and feeders. Hammered copper, molded resin, rustproof blends of cast iron and aluminum, and specially treated woods are only a few of the options available for adding year-round architectural features to the garden, patio, and terrace.

The wonderful variety seen in North American gardens results from both our diverse geographical and climatic regions, as well as our multiethnic heritage. Apart from the strong indigenous cultures of pre-Columbian Native America, we are a nation of immigrants who have drawn upon English and Continental prototypes and an ever-growing awareness of landscape design and furnishings from Latin America to the Mid- and Far East. In the early days, our principal exemplars were England, France, Spain, and the Netherlands. Then new waves of immigration brought growing influence from Italy, Germany, Scandinavia, Ireland, Portugal, Eastern Europe, and the Far East. The newcomers built homes and planted gardens in the styles familiar to them, adapting to the dictates of local climate and materials, and borrowing

freely from one another and from local Native American skills and plant lore.

Economics, of course, played a major part in garden size and function over time. The original stockaded enclaves in which crops were grown for subsistence, with herbs and flowers perhaps most valued for their healing and culinary properties, would evolve into farmsteads centered around a nearby community with its village green, as in New England, or its cobblestoned square with central fountain, in regions of Hispanic settlement. Such common spaces helped strengthen the emergent sense of community and set the tone for adjacent private gardens, which were cultivated mainly for vegetables, fruit, and other foodstuffs. Pleasure gardening did not become widespread until the eighteenth century, when many merchants, farmers, and Southern planters had become wealthy enough to pursue garden making as an avocation. A growing number of journals and house-pattern books with suggestions for landscape design helped the neophyte to experiment with fashionable ideas imported from Europe and to literally break new ground in creating traditional outbuildings like the wellhouse, springhouse, storage shed, and outdoor kitchen.

Decorative dovecotes, gazebos (also called summerhouses), geometric parterres edged with boxwood, espaliered fruit trees, and topiary trimmed in Classical modes took their places in Colonial and Early American gardens. Order and symmetry were the ruling principles, and the formal English garden, with its elaborate walled and fenced beds; avenues of stately trees lining the approach to the house and its perimeters; and straight-edged paths punctuated by Renaissance-style fountains and statuary retained its influence here long after gardeners in the Mother Country had turned to more naturalistic "landscape-style" design.

The American Gardener's Calendar, published in 1806 by Irish-American Bernard McMahon, was our first major landscape treatise, heralding the changes that were already well established in England and northern Europe. The transition to a freer, more parklike, landscape modeled on "nature unadorned" had first been adopted by the wealthy landed gentry for their great estates. Then English designers like Humphrey Repton and John C. Loudon adapted these concepts to the needs of the burgeoning middle class. At its grandest, the landscape garden comprised lakes and artfully channeled streams, Classical follies, meadows, vast terraces, newly planted "forests," and ha-has—moatlike depressions with sunken hedges or fencing designed to restrain straying livestock without impairing the view.

Independent American gardeners took a rather dim view of these developments until the 1840s, when designer and plantsman Andrew Jackson Downing published the first of his highly influential books, *A Treatise on the Theory and Practice of Landscape Gardening, Adapted to North America; with a View to the Improvement of Country Residences*. The salient phrase was "adapted to North America," and the impact of Downing's ideas was immediate and widespread. As Michael Weishan, the author of *The New Traditional Garden* (Ballantine, 1999), observes:

"Downing proposed that landscapes (and architecture) should strive to unify two essential characteristics: the *beautiful*, by which he meant the simple, classical, symmetrical, the *European*; and the *picturesque*—the stark, irregular, raw, *American*. In practical terms, this meant that he favored looser, more naturalistic planting areas that often derived their

Left: An imposing Victorian conservatory of ornate metalwork and glass, raised on a walled pavilion, rivals the famous Crystal Palace in splendor.

Introduction

Right: This cast-iron lidded vase with pedestal is an exemplar of the jardinieres made in the nineteenth-century Neoclassical style. It could be used as a freestanding ornament, or, with the lid removed, as a planter.

The prophet of the High Victorian-style garden was Frank J. Scott, author of *The Art of Beautifying Suburban Home Grounds* (1870), and its apostles included countless publications from *The Ladies' Home Journal* to *Vick's Illustrated Monthly Magazine*, *Burpee's Farm Annual*, and *Ornamental Gardening for Americans*. During this period, sight lines from the house commanded curving paths dotted with groups of graceful shrubs and weeping trees, wide pedestal urns overflowing with colorful flowers and vines, rustic gazebos, croquet lawns, gated stone stairways flanked by finials atop piers. Elaborate wrought- and cast-iron fencing and trelliswork echoed metal crestwork on the porch or the roofline, and sculpture groups varied from Classical muses and dryads to cherubs upholding fountains and bird feeders.

This era also saw the rise of mountain, lake, and seaside resorts, as middle-class families found it possible to take yearly vacations, or even to build a summer home in the country, with its "healthful airs" and scenic views. New York State's Catskill and Adirondack Mountains were highly favored; we continue to use Adirondack-style garden furniture that is sturdily made, comfortable, and as appropriate to certain garden styles as it was a hundred years ago. The picturesque maintained its hold on the popular imagination, and garden furniture, arbors, and summerhouses were constructed of twisted tree roots and branches, simple slats nailed to uprights on the diagonal, and rustic latticework, sometimes with a thatched roof or wire hoops supporting grapevines, clematis, and other popular climbers like Virginia creeper. Beachside houses in the Shingle style were often planted with native grasses, flowers, and

inspiration from the wild beauty of the new continent....His designs did contain beds, terraces, and other features with straight lines and geometric forms. But the parts of the garden were scattered about the landscape, the various features no longer held in strict relationship to one another—*only to the house.*"

That house may have been a venerable Georgian mansion, a Charleston townhouse, or one of the many new Gothic Revival, Italianate, and Tudoresque buildings that Downing himself helped to popularize, which were being constructed nationwide. His principles had nearly universal application and seized the imagination of the American garden maker. The way was open to a whole new approach that culminated in the lavishly ornamented Victorian garden of the post-Civil War era.

shrubs that could withstand the salt air, and furnished with castoff chairs and tables from the house repainted in bright colors like orange and blue.

The early twentieth century saw the pendulum swing back toward a more formal style in domestic architecture and gardening. The pre-eminent English garden designer of the late nineteenth century was Gertrude Jekyll, who reintroduced the large herbaceous border, planted in her own harmonious color schemes (she was a painter before her eyesight failed). She worked closely with the architect Sir Edwin Lutyens on many memorable gardens, including on her own property, Munstead Wood, in Godalming, Surrey. Here, older farmhouses and cottages inspired the use of native Bargate stone and local craft materials to create a dwelling that looked, by her description, "as if it had stood for 200 years." Its most striking feature was the south border, planted along a high stone wall, which was some 18 feet wide and 200 feet long.

Jekyll favored the use of architectural plant forms like the yucca and the acanthus and ornaments that were useful as well as decorative: the pergola as a showcase for climbing roses, the traditional sundial, weathered planters, and seating that was integral to the design. Like her contemporary William Robinson, Jekyll deplored the practice of carpet or ribbon bedding, whereby masses of annuals were planted out in soldierly rows and replaced every season. Her many books, including *Homes and Garden*, *Wood and Garden*, *Garden Ornament*, and *Gardens for Small Country Houses*, disseminated her ideas widely and were congenial with the Arts and Crafts movement aesthetic, which took root in the United States during the late 1800s.

The nation's potteries had been producing utilitarian redware for kitchen use, drain and roof tiles, and similar products for generations. But the new art pottery studios focused on creating decorative planters, tiles, birdhouses, fountains, and architectural faience in the Arts and Crafts style, which favored using natural "honest" materials and creating a handmade, appearance. Their use was especially prevalent in California and the Southwest,

Below: *A handsome stone lantern and a graceful curved bridge evoke the Far East in this tranquil water garden.*

Right: Native stone laid up as drywall remains popular for garden boundaries. Over time, mosses and creeping wildflowers help to emulate the timeworn look of old stonework like this example from Ireland.

where the climate allowed for year-round outdoor living. Other simply designed artefacts and hand-decorated objects from garden furniture to metalwork were adopted widely, and contemporary replicas have enjoyed a renaissance for the last several decades, from the Lutyens-style bench to a fluted flower-form garden bell inspired by Walter Crane's illustrations for the children's book *Flora's Feast: A Masque of Flowers.*

American architect and designer *extra-ordinaire* Frank Lloyd Wright was deeply influenced by the Arts and Crafts movement, although he firmly believed, and proved, that machinemade goods could be both authentic and beautiful when well designed and executed. His early Prairie Houses set new standards for domestic architecture, and their grounds were integral with the house, in keeping with his principle of organic unity. He sought to control every aspect of his projects so as not to compromise their integrity, and he carried this theme forward in the more compact Usonian houses of the 1930s and '40s, which often faced inward, away from the road, to provide outdoor living space that maximized privacy.

The rise of the Bungalow style, loosely based upon Far Eastern prototypes and carried to its apex by architects and landscape designers including the Greene brothers, Charles Sumner and Henry Mather, also reflected Arts and Crafts principles. More modest versions of this style, with deeply set porches on a single-story house, were constructed nationwide according to plans originating in Gustav Stickley's popular *Craftsman* magazine. Most of these houses had small, informal gardens dotted with native plants, like my grandparents' stucco retirement home in Miami, Florida, with its colorful hibiscus,

Left: A rugged pedestal of reddish stones mortared together supports this rustic birdbath in a lovely spring garden in North Milton, Prince Edward Island.

Above: *A rustic woven chair and an oval wall hanging echo the sheltering arches of a shaded enclave in the Hispanic mode.*

spiky palms, and fragrant night-blooming jasmine. It was a welcome sight—and scent—on our annual pilgrimage from the rigors of a western Pennsylvania winter during the 1950s.

The late nineteenth and early twentieth centuries also saw the construction of some of the most elaborate gardens ever conceived on these shores. The economy was robust, and vast fortunes had been made in mining, transportation, industry, and finance. Many of those fortunes were spent on creating lavish estates in a variety of Revival styles, from Neo-Colonial to English Manor, Chateauesque, Norman, Tudor, and Beaux Arts. Renaissance sculpture and furnishings graced formal gardens from Newport, Rhode Island, to Palm Beach, Florida. An army of laborers leveled a mountaintop near Asheville, North

Carolina, to create the Biltmore estate for George W. Vanderbilt, with its 250 rooms designed by Richard Morris Hunt overlooking a panoramic vista created by Frederick Law Olmsted, the nation's premier landscape designer. (An entire community near the gated entrance was relocated so as not to spoil the view.) Midwestern automobile production and Western shipping, mining, and timber gave rise to palatial houses and gardens that could be maintained only by cadres of groundskeepers in an era when labor was cheap and income tax was nonexistent.

World War II put an end to American gardening on this scale, and its aftermath saw a new low in landscape design, as tract housing sprang up to meet the needs of a growing postwar population and our major cities succumbed to urban blight in the wake of the flight toward the suburbs. Streamlined, angular Modernist housing did not lend itself to coherent, appealing garden decor, and expediency swept away many historic homes and districts in the name of progress. Subdivisions, shopping malls, and ill-conceived, mass-produced garden furnishings proliferated, and it is only in the recent past that our horticultural heritage has been renewed and restored to an appreciable degree. This trend has gone hand-in-hand with the growing awareness of our finite natural resources, the necessity for preserving the best of the past for new generations, and a rekindling of interest in handicrafts, folk art, vernacular architecture, and—above all—the joy of creating a personal environment that refreshes the spirit as well as the senses. The following pages give some idea of the rich possibilities inherent in traditional garden decor as adapted to the needs of the twenty-first century.

Decorative Planters & Trelliswork

Decorative planters helped to create the fabled Hanging Gardens of Babylon, and the Egyptians used large earthenware vessels planted with native trees in their formal gardens along the Nile. Urns, vases, even windowboxes, were made in Roman times, along with trelliswork that supported grapevines and other climbing plants. In Elizabethan England, boxwood-edged parterres, or knot gardens, accented by topiaries, were planted in symmetrical patterns that changed with the seasons, resembling intricate tapestries and richly woven carpets.

Rooted in agriculture, horticulture developed over the millennia as the primordial search for an elusive Garden of Eden, combining abundant fruiting trees and vines, shade- and shelter-giving plants, medicinal and culinary herbs, and a profusion of lush flowers cultivated for their beauty, fragrance, form, and contrast. Various climatic regions evolved gardens specific to their landscapes and native plants: the desert oasis fringed by exotic palms; the terraced Italian villa, dappled by the soft floral hues of the Mediterranean; enclosed courtyards cooled by fountains and brightened by luxuriant hanging and potted plants; serene Oriental temple gardens designed as windows on eternity to frame distant sacred mountains.

The European Renaissance drew upon the models of Classical antiquity—both real and imagined—to embellish pleasure gardens with ornamental planters made of terra cotta, stone, and marble in ever-more-elaborate designs. The latticed Versailles box, created in the seventeenth century by Andre Le Notre for the exquisite gardens of Louis XIV, remains a favorite to this day, although we no longer use it to create movable forests of fruit trees like those that were wintered over in the Sun King's orangery. Le Notre also

Opposite: *A Classical scalloped urn on a pedestal is encircled by azaleas at Rosedown, in St. Francisville, Louisiana.*

Left: *A bust of Shakespeare's Juliet framed by window sashes shows to even greater advantage with a living border of spring tulips.*

used imposing urns on pedestals to lead the eye down the long avenues of the formal gardens at Versailles. In a simplified form, this principle is still effective in defining walkways, low walls, and garden spaces devoted to various activities.

The two-edged sword of the Industrial Revolution cut away vast tracts of former farm- and pastureland in England even as it developed a host of new materials to enhance the built landscape: wrought iron, cast iron, composition stone, concrete, cast lead, and wood precut to standard lengths for construction purposes. Traditional earthenware of fired clay became available in many decorative shapes and sizes, from unglazed red or grey terra-cotta pots and urns to elegant tilework designed for the conservatories and garden rooms of great estates. New archaeological discoveries and the wideranging field work of dedicated landscapers contributed to our store of knowledge about historic gardens and their ornaments. Both landscape design

and architecture became increasingly respected professions, with a lively interchange of ideas and styles between Europe and the New World.

As prosperity increased, so did leisure time for the pursuit of pleasure gardening. It became a passion during the Victorian period (which, within North America, remained influential well into the early twentieth century). Householders ransacked pattern books and catalogues for "imperishable terra-cotta garden vases, palm holders, flower boxes, and tiled window boxes." Other containers in the popular "rustic style" were produced in wood with patterned palings or latticework. Like their ceramic counterparts, they were fitted with zinc liners.

French plant stands with scrolled wrought-iron bases and trellised wirework bowls were highly favored, as were wrought-iron stands with tiers of shelves designed to display choice plants from every angle. Rectangular cast-iron planters were molded with wreaths or garlands

Right: *Delightful topiary animals ornament a geometric parterre surrounded by colorful beds and borders at Bayou Bend, in Houston, Texas.*

and supported on footed bases in the form of acanthus leaves and other foliate designs. British manufacturers like Austin & Seeley produced composition-stone jardinieres molded in the form of flower trumpets, with petal-shaped rims, and basket-shaped planters of terra cotta with rolled rims and "woven" handles. The venerable design firm of Liberty & Company used many historic motifs on its gardenware, including Celtic knotwork, Tudor roses, and egg-and-dart detailing.

American potteries followed suit with their own distinctive designs, progressing from utilitarian redware and yellowware to salt-glazed stoneware urns, painted and glazed containers, and matte-glazed gardenware thrown and molded in naturalistic forms and decorated with flowers, birds, landscape silhouettes, rabbits, and stylized insects. Decorative tiles like those produced by Minton in England were manufactured from local clay by art potteries including California Faience, American Encaustic Tiling Company (AETCo), the Fulper Pottery, and the Grueby Faience Company. Both the Arts-and-Crafts aesthetic and Art Nouveau influenced their designs, which have become highly collectible in recent years. Faithful reproductions of these and other traditional garden ornaments are now widely available to American gardeners.

Renewed interest in topiary—the ancient art of sculpting growing plants into desired shapes—has produced many excellent books on the subject. One method involves training the plant to follow a framework, rather than cutting a large plant or shrub into an architectural or fanciful form. The latter method was more feasible for estate gardens tended by armies of laborers, while the trelliswork approach can be employed by any patient craftsperson. Topiary is especially popular for container gardening on small lots and in city gardens. You can purchase ready-made trellises in shapes ranging from hearts to crosses, cones, and obelisks, or create your own form with flexible wire

or supple branches bent and tied with twine. As the plant grows to cover the framework, it is trimmed and fastened until it achieves the desired shape. Suitable topiary plants include dwarf junipers, ivy, rosemary, myrtle, and miniature roses. Those that are not hardy can be brought indoors to brighten the winter months.

Espaliered fruit trees, trained to grow flat against a wall or fence, are another form of topiary, widely used during the late Middle Ages in the enclosed gardens of castles and monasteries. Today they create striking effects while optimizing the use of available space. Ornamentals like pyracantha, with its glossy leaves and berries, may be similarly trained, and their thorny branches provide both food and shelter for birds.

Very large pots containing topiary, weeping trees, or trellised vines are often used to frame an entryway or a vista. Such containers are now available in weatherproof materials like molded resin, or fiberglass with a faux-stone finish, which provide the appearance—but not

the weight—of antiquity. Insulating foam cores and self-watering devices contribute to the health of the potted plants and the gardener's peace of mind. Traditional terra-cotta pots of similar size and shape may serve to define garden rooms, stone walls, terraces, and other outdoor spaces. Garden designer Bunny Williams has used such containers astutely in her own Connecticut garden, which was described by Thomas Fischer of *Horticulture* magazine in the March 1993 issue:

"Plants growing in handsome terra-cotta pots play a major role....Carefully disposed throughout the garden, they complement the neat rows of vegetables and kitchen herbs, supplying color and interest when a group of lettuces or cabbages reaches its prime and disappears into the kitchen. They also provide a solution to the problem of what to do with tender herbs such as rosemary, which must be moved indoors for the winter, or biennials such as Canterbury bells, which have a spectacular but brief period of bloom. But most regal among the potted plants are the standards of bay, heliotrope, and osteospermum that Williams uses so liberally. Halfway between works of sculpture and products of nature, they occupy the most formal end of the garden's stylistic spectrum."

Small spiral or fan-shaped trellises add height and variety to container groups planted to provide the exuberance of a mixed border with the advantage of portability and easy reconfiguration. If annuals and perennials, including ornamental grasses, are combined for a colorful summer display, the perennials may be planted out at the end of the season. Rustic mini-trellises are easily made by interweaving flexible twigs that can be tied together to support a scented geranium or a top-heavy dahlia. Informal assortments of wooden boxes, half-barrels, and clay pots filled with annuals strike a welcome note beside a shingled New England-style cottage, and the plants are easily rotated for best sunlight

and blooms. On terraces and patios, whimsical pot risers in the form of frogs, flowers, or a variety of garden accessories help provide good drainage.

Figural cachepots and planters are available in every imaginable shape and form: contented cats, elegant swans, colorful roosters, serene Buddhas, Art Nouveau lilies, Chinese fishermen...the list would fill a book of its own. Wall planters, too, come in graceful, sophisticated designs that range from stylized wrought-iron vines with loops to support pots at various levels to multitiered half-rounds on scrollwork wall frames inspired by antique wirework. Fossil-stone planters with raised flourishes and ironwork supports command three-figure prices; far more affordable are painted to simulate weathering and fitted with sturdy steel rings. For the informal garden, galvanized-steel buckets can be painted in pastel colors to brighten a picket fence with cheerful African daisies (gerbera) or multihued petunias.

Left: A handmade trellis of pliable sticks graces a building at Broll Mountain Vineyards in California's Calaveras County.

Portable herb gardens are easily grown in lightweight troughs, or hexagonal pottery containers made of wedge-shaped sections that prevent the roots from invading each other. A sunny window box outside the kitchen is another way to enjoy the fragrance and convenience of fresh herbs, which are also pleasing to the eye in their various forms and colors. Some gardeners use such flowering herbs as chives, with their globe-shaped lavender blooms, to add interest to the perennial garden, but other species, like mint and dill, are too invasive for this purpose. They are better confined to raised beds or containers that prevent them from overrunning the neighboring plants. Gertrude Jekyll's ideas on the subject of herb gardens are as valuable today as they were a hundred years ago:

Below: A profusion of planters, vines, and hanging baskets fills the colorful forecourt of this Westport, Ireland, inn.

"Where house and garden are newly made, I like to arrange places for [the] herbs, not in the kitchen garden only, but so that there should be also close to the house, and somewhere near the door that gives access to the kitchen, a little herb garden for the cook....Here shall be two or three plants each of the Thymes, Basils, and Savories, Tarragon and Chervil, a bush of Sage, some clumps of Balm, Marjoram, and Fennel, Soup-celery and Parsley for flavouring, Borage, and a little Mint."

Thrift shops and garage sales can provide a delightful assortment of miniature flower holders to be grouped on a patio windowsill or outdoor shelf with one or two posies in each container. Tiny ceramic baskets, animals pulling flower carts, dollhouse hutches and chairs, chickens and watering cans, could all figure in such a

vignette, which is especially attractive to children. Playhouse windowboxes and special plots for easy-to-tend plants also nurture the universal fascination with growing things expressed so beautifully in Robert Louis Stevenson's *A Child's Garden of Verses.*

In these days when privacy is at a premium, both container plants and latticework can screen the yard from public view and contribute to the sense of enclosure in various outdoor spaces or "garden rooms." In his early Prairie houses, architect Frank Lloyd Wright frequently incorporated wide, shallow urns on pedestals into exterior designs that sheltered the main entrance from the street, creating a heightened sense of expectancy as one approached the house.

Woven lathing and trelliswork have been used since Colonial times to hide unsightly utility areas like compost heaps and toolsheds, as seen in historical restorations including Colonial Williamsburg, Virginia, and the properties maintained by the Society for the Preservation of New England Antiquities. Today we use such devices to conceal garbage cans, dog runs, and pumps for spas and swimming pools. Narrrow side yards can benefit from the addition of a trellis along the fence line, where trailing vines help shield the area from the view of neighbors. Exposed windows may be used to accommodate a greenhouse window that projects only a few feet from the house on lots too small for the addition of a modular greenhouse. Space permitting, a small greenhouse or conservatory enhances almost any garden, providing it is in keeping with the style of the house. There are innumerable attractive designs to choose from, whether you install a modular version or do much of the work yourself.

Visits to historic houses, botanical gardens, and arboretums in your area will provide a wealth of ideas on the use of decorative planters and trelliswork adaptable to your own garden style. The ever-increasing interest in conservation and restoration is also reflected in the work of local garden clubs and communal projects for inner-city beautification. In the recent past, gardening has regained its status as our Number One leisure activity, and there are few pleasures to compare with sharing ideas, experience, and favorite plants with other gardeners. Every season has its gratifications—and its disappointments—but as Henry David Thoreau reminds us, "Heaven is under our feet as well as over our heads."

Above: *A cottage-style garden in pots flanks the entry to this venerable brick dwelling, with its pentroof supports brightened by hanging baskets.*

Native Stone

The raised planting bed below, with its benches, paths, and stairways, seems to literally grow from its site in the skilled hands of masons from the Republic of San Marino, one of the world's smallest independent states. The native limestone, which has been quarried here for many centuries, features prominently in the local architecture and landscaping.

Another view of San Marino, opposite, leads the eye down a wide cobbled path flanked by terra-cotta pots to the vine-shaded entry of a two-story Mediterranean-style house with a wrought-iron balcony. Situated in central Italy on the slopes of Mount Titano, San Marino's long history of self-sufficiency has fostered a strong tradition of artisanship.

A Rustic Arbor *Opposite*

A charming latticed arbor and picket fencing open to a view of the country garden aptly named "Perennial Pleasures" in Prince Edward Island's Glen Valley—an idyllic setting on one of Atlantic Canada's most beautiful islands. With its rolling, green slopes, unspoiled coastline, and nostalgically preserved farmsteads, rural cottages, and picturesque villages, Prince Edward Island attracts visitors—including more than its share of garden fanciers—from around the world.

A Rose-Crowned Village Queen *Above*

Martha's Vineyard, Massachusetts, is well known as an enclave of Colonial charm, as seen in this view of a rose-bowered gateway opening to a clapboard house with a traditional garden.

Brimming with Color *Overleaf*

A half-barrel filled with multihued pansies draws attention to the rippling, rock-bordered stream that shimmers behind it (page 28). An old wine press serves as a uniquely appropriate ornament to the paved terrace of the Kautz-Ironstone Winery in Murphys, California (page 29).

A Rural Haven *Below*

Hanging petunias, snapdragons, railroad-sleeper boundaries, and a whimsical blue birdhouse with a miniature
shingled roof contribute to the relaxed ambience of
Garden City, in Rich County, Utah.

Harmonious Contrasts *Opposite*

The bountiful clematis vine in full bloom is the focal
point that unites the various elements of this charming
vignette: the curving slatted chair and footrest, weathered plank flooring, shingled wall, and latticework.

Patriotic Colors *Above*
Red, white, and blue sound the dominant notes at the doorway of a frame house in La Conner, Washington.

Out of Retirement *Right*
This old farm wagon has taken on new life as an unusual and imaginative raised flowerbed that highlights the grove behind this garden in Houston, British Columbia.

Grand Entrance *Previous pages*
A simple iron trellis laden with blooms opens to a view of the rose garden at McKinley Park in California's capital city, Sacramento.

Focused on Flowers *Below*
The forecourt cottage garden overflows with traditional climbing and bush roses and other old-fashioned favorites framed by white woodwork and reflected in a gazing ball.

To the Manor Born *Opposite*
A view of the walled tulip garden at the nation's grandest country house: the Biltmore estate in Asheville, North Carolina. Much of the landscaping for its rolling grounds was designed for Cornelius Vanderbilt II by Frederick Law Olmsted, the co-creator (with Calvert Vaux) of New York City's Central Park.

Cultivating the Natural Look *Above*

Handsome multilevel, meandering beds converge upon
an intricate latticed arbor hung with wind chimes and
colorful floral baskets in this charming garden at
Cornwall, Prince Edward Island.

My Lady's Fan *Below*
A classic fan-shaped trellis supports a rosarian's pride and joy in Sutter Creek, California, where the Gold Rush began in 1848. Many of the preserved towns in this area show the architectural and landscaping influences brought by more than 100,000 immigrants from the East Coast and Midwest in 1849–50.

Years in the Making *Overleaf*
This time-honored estate garden near the historic fort in Ticonderoga, in New York's Essex County, is a study in the skillful combination of plant materials, traditional masonry elements, and Classical ornament into a seamless whole. Colonial influences are still evident in the homes and gardens of this historic area.

An Informal Affair

The delightful montage of country crafts and found objects at left is a porch garden at the Route 97 Trading Post in Bend, Oklahoma.

Simplicity the Keynote *Below*

A sunburst of black-eyed Susans fringed with Queen Anne's lace invite a closer view of this idyllic country garden, with its rustic latticed arbor.

A Designer's Dream House *Above*
A vibrant blue façade, arabesque screenwork, and elegant plantings mark Yves Saint Laurent's retreat in exotic Marrakech, Morocco.

Oriental Grace *Right*
A wisteria trellis extends into the reflecting pool of the Japanese Garden at Seattle's Washington Park Arboretum, as the mounded azaleas in the foreground show their vibrant spring colors.

Garden Furniture & Lighting

The many styles and materials in period garden furniture today offer endless possibilities for creating outdoor rooms in keeping with the style and color of your house and the size of your property. Generally speaking, it is more desirable to acquire an eclectic collection of pieces you really love over time, rather than buying a whole "suite" of matching benches, tables, chairs, chaises, and so forth. However well made, such an assemblage offers little to the imagination and may obtrude upon the garden design rather than enhancing it in personal ways. Plastic woven to resemble white wicker will never look like the real thing, and its durability will do little to compensate for its lack of aesthetic appeal. In fact, white furniture of any type must be carefully chosen so that it doesn't detract from the garden's natural features, stopping the eye at the expense of ambient foliage, borders, and paths. A Colonial-style clapboard house, for example, is an ideal setting for a simple white deacon's bench that would look out of place in a contemporary townhouse garden. Sometimes a palette of more subdued colors, like moss green, grey, or black is more appropriate.

Wrought and cast-iron furniture in many period styles is now available with weather-resistant, powder-coat finishes that protect it from the elements. Even so, it should be wintered indoors in northerly climates if you plan to have years of use from it. However, unlike most wooden furniture, it is not susceptible to damage by fungi or termites. Suitable primers and paints will counter the danger of rust, caused by cracking of the surface coating when metal expands and contracts with the temperature.

Victorian and Regency-style metal furniture take many attractive forms. The rounded "conversation seat" may be assembled in a sinuous curve, with the seats facing in opposite directions, or side by side as a loveseat-sized bench embellished by simple scrollwork. Intricately patterned, nineteenth-century designs for cast-iron chairs and benches featured natural motifs including fern fronds, grapevines, morning glories, and passion flowers. Modern-day counterparts, some constructed out of lightweight coated aluminum, strike an elegant note in the period garden.

Antique "games seats" of wrought iron were fitted with wheels at one end for portability and equipped with folding footrests to protect long skirts and elegant boots from damp grass as the spectators followed badminton and court-tennis matches. The popularity of croquet lawns

Opposite: *A coach lamp wreathed in clematis brightens the entry to an old house clad in weathered siding.*

in Edwardian times also resulted in decorative benches, which were built with watertight lockers below the seats for storing the equipment. According to Michael Weishan, the author of *The New Traditional Garden* (Ballantine, 1999): "The popularity of croquet was such that hardly a landscape of distinction was designed during the last half of the [nineteenth] century that didn't prominently feature a croquet lawn. Public croquet teams and tournaments were formed all over the country, and results were followed with as much zeal as professional baseball or hockey is today. Such enthusiastic participation led to problems, however: in 1890s Boston, where the game was avidly played on Boston Common, the clergy felt the need to speak out against the drinking, gambling, and licentious behavior associated with croquet meets."

Rustic-style cast-iron chairs and benches modeled on wooden prototypes made from tree roots, vines, and branches were favored for nineteenth-century gardens influenced by Andrew Jackson Downing's ideas on landscape design—although they look desperately uncomfortable in the old catalogue illustrations. Should you acquire one of these antique cast-iron garden seats, you may choose to let it rust to a natural bronze patina and use it as a decorative feature only, surrounded by plantings in complementary colors.

Scrolled supports, arched, trellised, and slatted backs, and paw-shaped feet were typical of this period, as were curved "tree seats" designed to follow the contours of a tree trunk. The latter might take the form of a half-round, or encircle the tree completely, allowing a large party to enjoy the shade. Chairs and benches of French design, with decorative insets and delicate wirework, graced many American gardens and have recently been reinvented by contemporary suppliers of garden furnishings. They are especially attractive on the terrace or patio with small bistro-style tables for informal dining out of doors.

Wooden furniture in various styles has always been a favorite with American gardeners due to the abundant supply of fine hardwoods in the forests of the New World. When trade with China opened in the eighteenth century, English designers embraced all kinds of decorative objects "in the Chinese taste." Porcelains, carpets, lacquerware, and patterned fabrics modeled on exotic imports became immensely popular, and chinoiserie reigned in households with the taste and means to enjoy it. It found a still wider audience with the publication of William Halfpenny's pattern book *New Designs for*

Chinese Temples, Triumphal Arches, Garden Seats, Palings, etc. in 1750. (The reference to triumphal arches is probably to pagoda gates, which soon became a desirable architectural feature in the formal garden.) Straight-legged benches and chairs with fretwork (lattice-patterned) designs made their way into Colonial pattern books, and chinoiserie fences were used in fashionable Williamsburg, Virginia (now restored as Colonial Williamsburg).

The trend accelerated with the work of Thomas Chippendale, who established his cabinet-maker's workshop in London about 1748. Six years later, he published his influential furniture pattern book *The Gentleman and Cabinet Maker's Director.* His son Thomas succeeded him in the business, and their effect on garden-furniture design is still apparent in the versatile, clean-lined Chippendale bench and chair. The British writer Alistair Morris has illustrated many "Chinese Chippendale" revival designs from the nineteenth century in his book *Antiques from the Garden* (Garden Art Press, 1996). They include a wooden bench with slatted seat and back featuring arm supports with geometric fretwork decoration, and a more elaborate garden seat with an arched and slatted back and overscroll arms centered on roundels. It is similar in design to the teakwood bench and chair popularized by architect Edwin Lutyens, who collaborated with Gertrude Jekyll, during the early twentieth century. The Lutyens bench, too, is a garden-furniture perennial.

Durable (and expensive) teakwood is still in demand for rigorous conditions of use, including outdoor furniture and boat decking. A 1913 British catalogue offered a line of "Man-O'-War" garden seats made from the teak of retired navy ships, "which being thoroughly seasoned, is impervious to the effects of sun or rain, and requires neither paint nor varnish." Today, teak, cedar, and other wooden furnishings are usually given an oil finish to enhance their natural resistance to insects and rot, which is caused by fungi that flourish in humid conditions where the wood is in contact with the ground. Weathering also takes a toll, breaking down the surface cells of unprotected wood through ultraviolet (UV) rays from the sun. Once this occurs, the action of wind and rain literally erode the wood unless it is properly stained or painted. Other woods suitable for garden furniture include black locust, catalpa, redwood, sassafras, and white oak. However, except on paved areas, it helps to place

Left: A lantern like the one on the opposite page stands here on a stone pier framed by metal grillework.

stone or masonry footings under permanent garden benches, just as we use such footings to support the sills of sheds and other outbuildings for protection against rot. The same principle applies to built-in seating inside pergolas and summerhouses, which invites the visitor to rest in the shade or to enjoy a special vista.

An indigenous style is that of the Adirondack chair, which we associate with the rise of summer lodges and resorts in New York's Adirondack Mountains at the turn of the twentieth century. In fact, this popular design was introduced in 1905 as the Westport chair and bears little resemblance to the rugged, rustic creations in use at Adirondack "summer camps" during this period. The chair is roomy and comfortable, with wide arms to support drinks or reading material, and solidly based legs that do not sink into the

lawn. The angled and slatted back provides good support, and contemporary Adirondack furniture is made with stainless-steel hardware that will last as long as the wood without rusting. Durable cypress is a popular material, usually painted either green or white—sometimes allowed to weather to a muted silver-grey color. Adirondack-style pieces are appropriate in both traditional and contemporary settings.

Wooden furniture in the nineteenth-century rustic style is enjoying a revival, as seen in the form of willow and twig chairs and tables or benches made from tree trunks, roots, and branches—or facsimiles thereof. These nostalgic reminders of the Romantic movement in landscape design range from picturesque to fantastic, and they can be highly effective in woodland and meadow gardens. Cast-stone and resin composites, as well as wood and iron, have been used to create reproductions of this popular look.

Carved stone, including fine marble, benches date back to Roman times and were reprised in Europe beginning with the Italian Renaissance. Elegant marble, which ranges in color from pure white to grey, green, red, black, and other mottled colors, is actually limestone that is hard enough to take a polish. Other forms of limestone have also been used for garden seats and statuary, including Portland stone, from the British Isle of Portland. Soft when quarried, it hardens on exposure to the air. Antique examples from the nineteenth century are adorned with lions' heads, gryphon-shaped supports, and paneled backs with scrollwork and finials.

In the newly formed United States, stone benches and garden furnishings came into their own during the Greek

Right: A delightfully unexpected touch of garden decor—chairs covered in sphagnum moss and other natural materials in the snow-covered garden of Balthazar and Monica Korab in Troy, Michigan.

Revival period in architecture, in the early 1800s. Native marbles quarried in Vermont, and, later, in Southeastern states including Tennessee, Georgia, and Alabama, were used to produce straight-lined or curved benches in the Classical style. As they weathered, "cushions" of moss or lichen softened their lines and made them handsome focal points at the end of a path, or surrounded by flowering shrubs. Other types of building stone suitable for carving include limestone, which is easily cut and shaped with saws and planes, and granite, which is extremely strong but less workable. Stone's most important quality for garden use is density—the fewer pores or air cells it has, the less water it absorbs and the less susceptible it is to chipping and breakage under freezing conditions.

Contemporary garden seats in the Classical mode are usually made of cast concrete, or cast stone powder combined with fiberglass resin, which can be intricately detailed. Such pieces may be hand-finished to resemble Carrara marble and other traditional building stones and ornamented with acanthus leaves, fluting, dentils, and other features from the Classical orders—Doric, Ionic, and Corinthian. Garden suppliers also offer square-cut marble pedestals of varying heights and marble-topped tables for grouping on terraces and patios. Similar accessories may be found at local yard sales and flea markets and refinished to your taste—a less expensive option that is also fun to experiment with. They help to create an Italian feeling in a garden room, which is especially attractive in hot, arid regions of the country. The American novelist Edith Wharton was inspired by her European travels to write *Italian Villas and Their*

Gardens (1904), which vividly describes the charm of Mediterranean landscaping:

"The Italian garden does not exist for its flowers; its flowers exist for it: they are a late and infrequent adjunct to its beauties, a parenthetical grace counting only as one more touch in the general effect of enchantment. This is no doubt partly explained by the difficulty of cultivating any but spring flowers in so hot and dry a climate, and the result has been a wonderful development of the more permanent effects to be obtained from the three other factors in garden composition—marble, water and perennial verdure—and the achievement, by their skillful blending, of a charm independent of the seasons."

Seldom seen nowadays, but a fascinating footnote to the history of garden furnishings, are the earthenware or glazed-pottery seats produced in the mid- to late nineteenth century, notably by several British manufacturers. Minton made brightly glazed and decorated garden seats

Left: A natural sculpture of timber rounds has been sprinkled with snowlike petals from an overhanging apple tree in this corner of the Korabs' four-acre garden. Sculptures like this can be designed as informal outdoor tables or seating.

Above: *Decorative Victorian-style garden furnishings have found a congenial home on the grounds of Auburn (1812) in Natchez, Mississippi.*

including a crouching monkey supporting a tassel-trimmed cushion, and an hourglass-shaped seat designed by architect A.W.N. Pugin in royal-blue Majolica with stylized strawberry plants and Gothic tracery in white, yellow, and red. Doulton offered a glazed stoneware garden seat supported by sphinxes with upswept wings that formed the arms of the bench.

A handsome terra-cotta chair advertised as an Etruscan design from the Palazzo Corsini in Rome was made by Italy's Manifattura di Signa in the early twentieth century. The seat was decorated with Classical figures and foliate forms, with a gracefully flared back, resting on a short tapering column of the same mellow color. American potteries, too, offered a variety of gardenware ranging from the utilitarian flower pot to hand-decorated ornamental tiles inspired by the Arts and Crafts movement. Majolica garden seats

and tables are also available in well-made reproductions that are remarkably faithful to the original designs.

Garden lighting, once limited largely to torches, lanterns, and candles, has evolved into an art form in its own right. Subdued electric lighting in the form of spotlights concealed under the eaves of the house, or behind plantings, can highlight selected garden features, illuminate paths, and contribute to the sense of privacy and seclusion. When the garden is under snow, its winter beauty can be enjoyed from the comfort of the house.

Diffused lighting, which makes use of translucent materials like fiberglass, can be installed overhead in wall panels on the terrace, and underwater lighting enhances the nighttime enjoyment of ornamental ponds and swimming pools. Lotus-shaped floating candleholders create a beautiful effect on these water features as well. Chinese and Japanese paper lanterns, as depicted in John Singer Sargent's Impressionist painting *Carnation, Lily, Lily, Rose* (1885), have retained their popularity as soft illuminants that lend a festive air to the outdoor scene for special occasions.

Another "wireless" possibility is the use of solar accent lights to define flowerbeds, decks, and pools. They come on automatically at dusk, radiating a peaceful, candlelike glow. Recharged by partial sunlight, they shine for up to eight hours by means of efficient solar cells.

Outdoor fireplaces are being used in imaginative ways as the focal points for patios and courtyards, especially in the West. They may be attached to the outside wall of a house, or serve as freestanding garden hearths. Smooth river rocks, slate tiles, and terra-cotta pavers make attractive surrounds for these architectural features, which often have built-in seating and privacy walls. The San Diego-area landscape architect Steve Adams has designed several prize-winning installations, including a slate-tiled courtyard dug into a steep hillside at a house in Del Mar, California. The bold rectangular chimney of the fireplace doubles as a retaining wall, partially faced with river rocks and surrounded by luxuriant tropical plantings.

The free-standing Mexican *chimenea*, or earthenware outdoor fireplace, also makes a striking feature that radiates warmth and light. The traditional form is that of a large vase supported on a masonry or metal-legged base. Dramatic contemporary designs may be fish- or dragon-shaped. The adobe *horno*, a beehive-shaped outdoor oven long used in the Southwest, is another attractive option for informal terrace and patio use.

A wide array of garden torches and lanterns is available, from tabletop size to in-ground stakes of mahogany, copper, and iron supporting glass globes. Some are fueled by kerosene or lamp oil, others by insect-repelling citronella oil or candles. More than a century after its introduction, the hurricane lantern remains a popular garden ornament and lighting fixture. Originally developed for the use of railwaymen, it was named for the fact that the flame was so well protected that not even a hurricane could blow it out. Contemporary versions are produced in heavy-duty painted metal and glass. They emit a twelve-candle-power light using lamp oil or kerosene and burn for twenty-four hours or more without refueling. As a safety feature, the light goes out automatically if the lantern

tips over. Hardworking railway signal-men also called this the blizzard lantern.

Chinese lanterns in the eighteenth-century style, made of glazed ceramic or ornamental ironwork, make elegant shadows on the garden wall when used as candleholders. A formal look is created by massive brass candlesticks with pierced Moorish-style decoration and antiqued verdigris finish, which support short, pillar-shaped candles. Delightful effects are also created by pierced votives in the form of animals and plants, which have a small door in back for inserting the candle. Ornamental fixtures, including sconces, affixed to garden walls make an architectural statement.

The possibilities for furnishing and illuminating your garden with pieces inspired by timeless designs from around the world are almost limitless, as the following plates will illustrate.

Below: An unusual antique lamp of metal and glass mounted in a fluted column is the ideal complement to this brick-walled terrace with multilevel plantings at Riveroaks in Austin, Texas.

Scrollwork and Floral Forms *Opposite and below*

Two fine examples of metalwork garden furnishings: on the opposite page, an airy wirework gazebo painted white contrasts with darker metal furniture and fencing at the Almaden Vineyard in San Jose, California; below, elaborate French-style furniture with a rose motif shows to even greater advantage against a background of flowering dogwood in Sutter Creek, California.

Neo-Norman Style *Overleaf*

The striking Souverain Winery building and grounds in Sonoma County, California, are lineal descendants of the great Norman chateaux of France. Note the strong vertical lamppost in the foreground, which echoes the steep line of the dormered tower with its flaring eaves.

Patriotic Inspiration *Above*
This delightful rustic bench, long since painted red,
white, and blue, has a place of honor outside the post
office in Gandy, Nebraska.

A Sculptural Presence *Below*

The distinctive cast-concrete bench below has the look of a Lutyens piece, with its arched back and flaring armrests. The slotted openings provide for cooling air circulation and rainwater runoff. Note how the delicate floral tracery lightens the appearance of this substantial seat.

A Rustic Hideaway *Above*

An unusual pergola anchored by evergreens frames a woodland enclave furnished with two hammocks and a green Adirondack chair in the country garden "Perennial Pleasures"at Glen Valley, Prince Edward Island.

Indoor/Outdoor Living *Opposite*

Cream-colored rattan furnishings overhung by an arbor of white wisteria help to create a sun-dappled outdoor room beautified by massed containers of delicate Angelique tulips.

Shades of Summer *Overleaf*

Brightly painted wooden chairs and tables and a simple bench under the far window complement the lines of the wooden railing and cast slatted shadows on the wall of this spacious porch in California's Amador County.

A Simple Resting Place *Below*

An unobtrusive antique chair invites the visitor to stop and view the gnarled trees, greensward, and day lilies at the Historical Society Gardens on Deer Isle, Maine.

A Venerable Artefact *Opposite*

The time-honored stone lantern opposite, with its pierced and embossed decoration, marks the way through the evocative Japanese Garden in Washington Park, Portland, Oregon. The humid climate of the Pacific Northwest is congenial to azaleas and other plants native to the Orient.

Japanese Lanterns *Previous pages*
On page 66, a pagoda-roofed lantern points the way
over an arched cobblestone bridge in the Washington
Park Arboretum's Japanese Garden. On the facing page,
bamboo fencing frames a sculptural symbol of enlightenment at the Heian shrine in Kyoto.

Sturdy Stoneware *Below*
A simple composition-stone bench on rough-hewn legs
makes a pleasing contrast to the greenery around it.

Unusual Accents *Above*
Adirondack-style chairs with Gothic points and finials
along the top form an eye-catching vignette at "Perennial
Pleasures" in Glen Valley, Prince Edward Island.

Southern Elegance *Overleaf*
Handsome cast-iron Victorian benches flank the brick
stairway of an impressive symmetrically designed terraced garden in Natchez, Mississippi.

Setting a Standard *Opposite and below*

The ornate antique fixture opposite, with its moonlike globes clustered on Victorian scrollwork supports, draws attention to the bank of roses surrounding it and to the eclectic nineteenth-century Placer County, California, courthouse. The pebbled-glass lantern on a fluted supporting column, below, stands in the Zilker Botanical Garden in Austin, Texas.

Architectural Perfection *Opposite*
The intricate brickwork, triple-tiered fountain, and wrought-iron gate with palmetto motif are enhanced by the glowing lantern that casts its light over a secluded garden in Columbia, South Carolina.

A Rustic Gazebo *Below*
A conical timber framework overgrown with vines shades a simple seating arrangement of wooden chairs and benches for outdoor enjoyment in this garden in Prince Edward Island.

Paths & Borders

The features that bind your garden into a coherent whole are the paths and borders that make it a self-contained extension and enhancement of your home. For example, if your site is on steeply falling ground, it may be preferable to follow the terrain with a multilevel terraced yard united by paths or paving than to move a ton of earth to create a limited, dead-level space that could end up resembling a bunker. High-level decks are often used on such hilly sites, with mixed results. One disadvantage is that almost nothing will grow beneath them, so the space at ground level is virtually thrown away. With a modicum of planning, you can create a terraced yard with well-defined spaces for outdoor dining, children's play, and planting areas laid out on the "circle in a square" model, centered on a reflecting pool or sundial. The area might be bordered by a privacy screen of latticework softened by evergreen or annual vines, or perhaps clematis. When in doubt, the simplest (and least expensive) solution may well be the best.

Many suburban houses have ample frontage and lend themselves to the creation of a forecourt whose focal point is the entrance to the house. Garden designer Maryanne Binnetti points out in her book *Shortcuts for Accenting Your Garden* (Storey Communications, 1993) that the same rectangular, gable-roofed house with a central entrance can take on entirely different looks according to the landscape style used. For example, instead of having two rectangles of lawn split by a cement path to the doorway, you might consider a more traditional approach that draws upon, but scales down, the symmetrical formal style. This could include a curving path of brick laid in a herringbone or running-bond pattern, with round, brick-edged island beds halfway to the entrance on either side. Foundation plantings scaled to the house—perhaps clipped pyramidal evergreens at each corner, with rounded evergreens below window level—and a brightly painted door would complete this attractive approach, equally suitable for a Colonial, Victorian, or country-style house. Neat hedging along both sides provides a border and a backdrop for specimen trees and other plantings without obscuring the view from the street.

The same modest house takes on an entirely different ambience if the dooryard is planted in the country-cottage style. A path of random flagstone or bluestone, window boxes overflowing with flowers, a birdbath underplanted with pansies or clematis would all be appropriate here. Off-center, free-form flower

Opposite: Old brick laid in a crosshatch pattern and bordered by marigolds and begonias makes an attractive approach to this multigabled California home.

beds and a picket fence with an arched trellis leading to the back yard help to create a space that is well-defined, but not cramped-looking. Good boundaries lead the eye toward the next vista and create a sense of expectancy.

If you favor an uncluttered Oriental look, the front yard might focus on a staggered walkway of round stepping stones, several handsome trees—perhaps cut-leaf maples or rounded evergreens—groups of low-growing azaleas as foundation plantings, and a stone lantern bordered with smooth river rocks and clumps of ornamental grasses. Fine sand can be raked to suggest a stream of water around an ornamental feature, as seen in the traditional Japanese or Zen garden.

The naturalistic or woodland style is a perennial favorite with country garden-ers and especially well suited to shingled houses or those with stained wood siding. Here, pathways lined with wood chips or pebbles contained by low edgings are appropriate, along with informal groups of ferns and native plants. A hollow stump can be converted into an asset by planting it with cheerful annuals that flourish with little care. Folk-art decor like whimsical handmade birdhouses, and found objects including antique farm tools, are popular decorative features; so are rustic trellises fashioned of grapevine or pliable branches. The low-maintenance feature of this style is especially appreciated for vacation homes, and the surrounding woodlands blend seamlessly into the garden.

Southwestern houses of adobe and stucco lend themselves to Mediterranean-style landscaping, which was developed for hot climates with infrequent rainfall. Drought-resistant native plants like cacti and succulents will thrive where most others would fail. Instead of grass, tiling, stone flags, or fine gravel can serve not only for pathways, but as the main surface material. Adobe walls and informal wooden fencing are both effective for bordering this type of yard, which has the advantage of being water-conservative. A similar approach works well with Western-style ranch houses, even where the climate is not arid. Rugged boulders accented by a spiky blue-green yucca or a colorful piece of folk-art pottery need not be confined to the Sun Belt. To avoid a barren look, the Mediterranean landscape benefits by exuberant container plantings or beds of blazing color—double poppies, bright-orange geum, golden calendula, scarlet geraniums, and other favorites in this spectrum.

Below: An eclectic Victorian house in historic Georgetown, Colorado, gains added appeal from its overflowing windowboxes, edgings, and container plantings in vibrant primary colors accentuated by white flowers that complement the ornate "gingerbread" house trim.

Dedicated rosarians can create a formal rose garden along one or both sides of the front yard, perhaps linked to an informal back-yard display of favorite bushes and climbers by white or natural-color lattice-work. Historically, we have looked to Great Britain for guidance in both the cultivation and decorative uses of these beautiful flowers, as seen at much-admired National Trust gardens including Hidcote and Sissinghurst. However, you need not have a landed estate to enjoy a preponderance of roses, accented by such traditional companions as iris, artemisia, phlox, and heather. A rose garden is especially appropriate to the concept of "garden rooms" formed by hedging and mellow brick or stone walls. It is also enhanced by a shallow central reflecting pool surrounded by simple pavers.

Since children have a deep affinity with nature, you may wish to consider a play area that includes colorful (and durable!) plantings that they can help to tend. A variety of safe and attractive furnishings for such an area is available, from treehouses and playhouses to swing sets, wading pools, and climbing frames. The playhouse could be provided with window boxes in which pots are easily rotated through the season, and flowers like marigold that are easily grown from seed will encourage the universal fascination with the process of growth. Raised vegetable beds can serve the same purpose, with a small plot assigned to each family member for sowing, weeding, and harvesting. The playground garden should be visible from the house for supervision—perhaps adjacent to the patio—and attractive enough to serve as a working part of the landscape.

Ideally, your garden-decor scheme (or makeover) will begin in the front yard

and focus on the doorway as a welcoming feature. Questions to be asked here include: Is the walkway wide enough for the scale of the yard? Is the paving material consistent with the style of the house? Do the foundation plantings need pruning, or even replacement? Many neophyte gardeners neglect to read the tags on nursery stock and triumphantly carry home an assortment of trees and shrubs that will triple in size within a few years' time, shading out the front windows and

Above: On Martha's Vineyard, Massachusetts, an elegant fence with architectural columns and closely spaced palings barely contains the luxuriant border behind it.

79

creating an overgrown tangle that all but conceals the house. Such plantings can also cause structural damage through invasive root systems and pressure on gutters that divert water from the house. Clearing out unwanted growth along the foundation and repainting the front door in a bold color can make an immediate improvement, especially if a group of attractive container plantings is added to enhance the entryway.

Decisions on paving materials will also carry over to the side and back yards to ensure that complementary "hardscaping" adds cohesion to the design. Cost, of course, is a major consideration, including the installation factor. Can you do the work yourself, or will you need a contractor? This depends on the type of paving you choose and the complexity of the job, both considerations that also apply to walls and fencing.

In some areas, including in New England, weathered, flat fieldstone is still widely available for paths, borders, and terraces and is easily seated by incorporating sharp builder's sand into the underlying soil. Drywall—laid up without masonry—is extremely attractive and can be built by the amateur mason with a good guidebook. New England is still criss-crossed by miles of old stone walls erected by early settlers, who marked their boundaries and contained livestock with the stones laboriously dug from their fields in the process of clearing a homestead. Random-sized stones also make popular informal edgings for flower beds and borders.

Bluestone, available at most garden centers by the foot or yard, takes longer to acquire a mellow, worn look, which can be facilitated by occasional applications of buttermilk. Most landscapers favor the

Right: Here is a rare example of skillful multilevel plantings, including a wall of flowering rhododendron and azaleas bordered by a low, dense hedge at Shore Acres State Park, in Coos City, Oregon.

slate-blue variety over the reddish blue-stone, because it looks better with flowers and foliage, whether interplanted among the stones or used in a border. Another alternative is the use of granite cobbles, called "setts," which paved our cities' streets a century and more ago. They came here as ballast in empty trading ships from Europe and can be seen in old photographs of long-settled cities like New York and Boston. They made for a bumpy carriage ride, but were far preferable to having the streets churned into a sea of mud in wet weather. Millions of these cobblestones were eventually overlaid with asphalt, but you may be lucky enough to buy some if a nearby street is torn up. Otherwise, they are ruinously expensive, although they make an incomparable surface for planted terraces laid with close joints, and for courtyard paving in elegant private houses in various period styles.

The finest grade of gravel, called peastone, forms handsome paths when suitably contained and is an ideal medium for establishing delicate plants in rock gardens. Coarser grades of gravel from the stoneyard are usually mixed with fine particles of clay or sand and will take on a different texture and color when washed by rain. Some authorities recommend purchasing a small quantity of such gravel and hosing it off at home to see how it will look in your setting before you make a decision. It is not ideal as a terracing medium, because weeds grow through it with undiminished vigor. Coarser gravel is also less comfortable underfoot than peastone, and crushed stone dust, which packs as hard as cement with wear, should be used only for driveway surfacing.

Small white marble chips can be used effectively in creating island beds, or to provide the appearance of a stream running through a Japanese-style garden. It is also useful for creating a rock-bordered artificial pool, perhaps with a graceful bird or animal sculpture "drinking" from it. Like fine sand, it can be raked into patterns, and small arched bridges over such simulated water features have been used to pleasing effect. However, thorough drainage is essential to keeping such decorative elements in pristine condition.

Factory-made bricks, like mass-produced flowerpots, will never have the same look as the antique kiln-fired originals. However, they will weather over time and

Above: *Antique kiln-fired brick paving in a herringbone pattern defines the structure of this English-style formal garden in historic Ticonderoga, New York, the site of a Revolutionary War fortress.*

can be laid in a variety of attractive patterns to form both walkways and walls. Brick piers on either side of a gate lend importance to an entryway, especially when crowned with planted urns or bold finials: stone pineapples, spheres, and obelisks are all traditional forms for this usage. Garden and shelter magazines are filled with good ideas for the incorporation of such features into your landscape. However, it is essential to use brick produced especially for outdoor use, and to have it laid close on pathways to avoid a scraggly look and heaving in winter frosts. Many-shaded antique brick can sometimes be acquired (at considerable cost) from salvage and housewreckers' yards and laid up by a skilled mason to last for years, with proper coping along the tops of walls to prevent moisture damage.

Below: A mound of brilliant red azaleas draws the eye to the geometric stone slabs leading to the entrance gate of the Tea Garden at the beautiful Japanese Garden in Portland, Oregon's, Washington Park.

Brick terraces, if they are to be planted, may be laid closely in panels, with occasional spaces to serve as flower beds for creeping plants. Alternatively, low brick or concrete walls enclosing the terrace can be designed to incorporate both seating and container plantings. New techniques for staining concrete in warm, diffuse colors have made it possible to use this practical material in traditional settings. Reinforced concrete retaining walls may also be clad in brick or other facing materials for stability and economy. Versatile poured concrete was first used effectively in buildings and landscaping by European architects and, in this country, by Frank Lloyd Wright, at the turn of the twentieth century. Its bold sculptural quality lends itself to traditional as well as modern architecture in the hands of a skilled designer.

Often, a combination of paving materials is surprisingly effective. Landscaper Wayne Winterrowd, in an article for *Horticulture* magazine (February 1992), observes that "The most delightful terrace I ever saw was composed of slabs of aged bluestone with panels of brick worked in, laid sometimes in herringbone pattern, sometimes in basketweave, and sometimes in running bond. The whole was eked out with an occasional granite sett or well-shaped fragment of fieldstone, and the joints—which were sometimes five inches wide—were filled with gravel. The result was charming, suggestive both of medieval spontaneity and of thrifty New England making do."

Borders of various kinds "frame" your garden pictures and help to create minivistas within the broader outline. This requires the use of linear features including fences, shrubs, and screening, not only for privacy and boundary definition, but to create garden rooms or sections. The decorative kitchen garden or potager, for example, has become an increasingly popular form of garden art, uniting the functions of pleasure gardening with the production of fresh, organic produce for the table. The indispensable unifying element is a series of clean, well-defined masonry paths and such border material as clipped yew or hornbeam, which provides wind protection and the required sense of enclosure. These features unite the various herb and vegetable beds, which change from season to season. Vegetables for such a garden could contain cabbages (including the feathery, multicolored ornamental varieties), leeks, parsnips, potatoes, Brussels sprouts, and celeriac, as well as the usual lettuce, tomatoes, runner beans, and spinach. Pots on pedestals, planted with miniature citrus trees or fragrant flowering herbs, provide vertical accents in a well-planned, productive potager.

The enhancement afforded by appropriate boundaries can be seen along a continuum ranging from the elegant wrought-iron fencing that encloses a showplace in New Orleans' Garden District to the style and material of decorative edgings for your flower beds. Whether composed of natural stones, mini-pickets, bricks laid on edge, or decorative metal hoops and finials with recurring motifs, these "outlines" should be consistent with your garden style and placed to lead the eye effortlessly from one vignette to another. Living borders like hedgerows and flowering shrubs may be combined effectively with latticework, low walls, irregular stones, timbers, adobe, or any other suitable material.

A natural feature like a boulder too large to remove may be transformed into the focal point of a pocket garden of native plants, lit indirectly and visible from the house by day or night. A storm-damaged tree may give place to a still more flourishing specimen in years to come, and half a dozen cherished rosebushes planted in an octagonal bed edged with bricks may give you as much pleasure as an acre of roses in a landmark botanical or estate garden. Fortunately, such is the camaraderie of dedicated gardenmakers from every walk of life that they will go on sharing experience, ideas, choice plants, and decorative schemes as long as there is a bare spot in need of refurbishing or a new spring alive with fresh possibilities.

Above: Another view of the hedged formal garden at Ticonderoga, New York, its colorful parterres accented by conical evergreens. Note the "window" cut into the hedging in the background to give a glimpse of the landscape beyond — a feature typical of English estate gardens.

A Well-Planned Gravel Path *Above*

Suitably contained by edging, a path of fine gravel can
be as effective as this example in the Japanese Garden
in Portland's Washington Park. Without edging, the
gravel would soon be scattered beyond its boundaries.

A Stone Quarry Reborn *Previous pages*

Vancouver Island's incredible Butchart Gardens, decades
in the making, were created in an abandoned quarry
near the center of the historic city of Victoria.

Countless Shades of Green *Below*
At Thuya Gardens, in Northwest Harbor, Maine, soothing shades of green subtly emphasized by flowering
plants comprise a true study in serenity, recalling the
poetic line "a green thought in a green shade."

A Naturalistic Woodland Garden *Page 88*
Weathered wooden palings are the ideal backdrop for this seemingly artless, but carefully composed border in a Charlottetown garden on Prince Edward Island.

A Spine of Stone *Page 89*
Note how the uncut stones descending from the ornamental lantern serve to unify the diverse colors and forms of the lovely plants in this early-summer garden on Washington State's Vashon Island.

Path to Enlightenment *Above*
Stone slabs and random-size rocks form this symbolic pathway to the Ryoanji Temple in Kyoto, Japan, which is trodden with reverence for the unity underlying the apparent diversity of all things.

A Gradual Descent *Opposite*
Unobtrusive natural materials comprise this handsome walkway, eminently suitable to The Ledges in Northwest Harbor, Maine. Visits to such show gardens are a valuable source of ideas and adaptations for your own special place in the sun.

Still Waters *Below*

For those who feel that no landscape is complete without a pool or pond, the shallow Japanese garden pool below, surrounded by natural boulders and flowering azaleas, provides quiet satisfaction.

A Secluded Oasis *Above*
A tranquil ambience pervades the Natural Garden in Portland's Japanese Garden, where stone slabs form a walkway past the rock-studded pool.

Surprised by Spring *Page 94*
This flowering tree in the Berkshires of Massachusetts appears as a cloud of bloom rising from the rough stone wall framed from New England's rugged hills.

At Home on the Range *Above*
A rustic fence near Willow City, Texas, is embedded in colorful wildflowers. Weathered wood blends harmoniously into its surroundings when used in fencing for rural yards.

A Walk Through the Hermitage *Page 95*
Swordlike iris leaves of green edged in gold reflect the sun-dappled blossoms overhead along this neatly edged gravel path through The Hermitage, President Andrew Jackson's beloved home in Nashville, Tennessee.

A Private Sanctuary *Below*

A curving brick path leads the eye through this well-tended informal garden in Milton, Prince Edward Island, to the lattice-topped slatted wooden fence and garden gate that is finished with a mirroring curve.

A Woodland Garden *Overleaf*

Broad steps of smooth slabs of stone and random paving softened by creeping moss seem carved from this scenic hillside, which is beautifully planted with flowering shrubs and small trees.

A Stately Panorama *Page 100*
This comprehensive view of the estate garden at Ticonderoga, New York, takes in the imposing architectural features, deep borders, brick paving, and the broad sweep of lawn, with its Chippendale-style bench beneath a shade tree.

Raised Stepping Stones *Page 101*
These symbolic stepping stones rise from the lily pond of the Shinto shrine Heian, in Kyoto, Japan.

Mid-May Splendor *Left*

The terrace of the hipped-roof mansion at Lakewold in Tacoma, Washington, is wreathed in wisteria vines trained to the openwork trellis supports, forming a living border for this porch. Substantial container plantings are in keeping with the scale of the house.

An Elegant Memorial Garden *Below*

The Garden Club of Georgia is responsible for this tasteful memorial to the founders of the University of Georgia at Athens, established in 1857. A sundial is placed at the center of the mazelike pattern of paths and hedging.

Incandescent *Opposite*

The incredible fall colors of the Japanese maple light up the serene lakeside, with its organically blending overhanging deck, of the Japanese Gardens at Seattle's Washington Park Arboretum.

A Contemplative Retreat *Below*

Hand-tied bamboo fencing opens to the simple screened Tea House framed by Japanese maples in fall color at the Washington Park Arboretum. The nineteenth-century immigration of skilled gardeners from the Land of the Rising Sun to our Pacific Coast brought a whole new concept of garden art to the United States.

A Natural Rock Wall *Overleaf*

Softly colored rock plants including lupines and valerian clothe a naturally occurring rugged stone border that forms a wall. A similiar effect can be achieved with boulders in a split-level garden.

Random Paving and Rock Borders *Page 107*

An informal path of stone slabs and irregular rocks and a rough-hewn stone wall are eminently suited to this naturalistic woodland garden in the Pacific Northwest.

A View from the Bridge *Below*

A traditional Japanese Moon bridge spans a pristine
stream rimmed by mounded green and flowering shrubs.

Enrobed in Flowers *Above*

The brilliant pink of luxuriant azaleas conspires with delicate fern fronds to soften this simple rock boundary.

British Columbian Treasure *Overleaf*

Landscape design and civic pride join hands at Vancouver's immaculately groomed Queen Elizabeth Park. Simplicity and scrupulous, regular maintenance are the keynotes in these attractively shaped borders and the unobtrusive walkway and bridge.

109

Luxuriant Plantations *Above and opposite*
The long sultry summers of the lower Mississippi Valley
led residents to create cooling scenes like the one at
Louisiana's Hodges Gardens (above) and the shaded
forecourt of Green Leaves (right), built in Natchez,
Mississippi, in 1838. Low-level plantings soften the lines
of this straight stone pathway.

The Cottage Garden *Page 112*
Neat white picket fencing encloses a cheerful cottage
garden traversed by a grassy path in Standish, Maine.

Focal Point *Page 113*
A graceful fruit tree thickly underplanted with white flowers presides over the naturalistic landscape in this New
Brunswick garden, which is framed by a neat, traditional-
style picket fence.

On the Natchez Trace *Above*

Cherokee Gardens, one of the many gracious prebellum estates in Natchez, Mississippi, has a handsome circular forecourt with formal parterres centered on the short fluted pedestal that supports the wrought-iron armillary. The neat stone edging unites these features with the path and driveway.

Sedimentary Rocks *Page 116*

Irregular steps of sedimentary rock flanked by a section of New England drywall form a pleasing approach to this grove in the Berkshires, western Massachusetts.

The French Influence *Opposite*

French settlers left their imprint throughout the Mississippi Valley, as seen in the formal garden fronting the Henri Penne House in St. Martin Parish, Louisiana.

Inviting a Closer Look *Page 117*

A winding natural-effect path edged by liriope and flowering shrubs gives a distant glimpse of the gazebo at Rosedown, in St. Francisville, Louisiana.

Shades of André Le Notre *Above*

The imposing terrace at Afton Villa, with its tightly
clipped parterres and topiaries opening into the parklike grounds beyond it, recalls the great gardens of
Versailles created by the eminent French landscape
designer André Le Notre.

Simplicity Sets the Scene *Overleaf*

Andrew Jackson's unpretentious taste is reflected in the simple design of the garden that he created as a refuge from the pressures of political life: The Hermitage, in Nashville, Tennessee.

Dunleith Garden, Natchez *Below*

Weathered antique brickwork frames the geometric parterres at this Southern estate garden, built about 1855 by C.C. Dahlgren on land inherited from his father-in-law and first planted in the late eighteenth century.

Reaching for the Sky *Page 123*

Gertrude Jekyll would have delighted in this exuberant perennial garden, structured by a high wall with climbing plants and overhung with cascades of flowers on a hilly site in Seattle, Washington.

Timeless Appeal *Pages 124-5*

Clouds are reflected in twin pools framed by weathered timbers in the foreground of this landscape garden at Bellingrath estate in Mobile, Alabama. Though it appears to date from an earlier era, the 60-acre site was designed during the 1930s in a harmonious blend of Colonial, English, and Mediterranean influences.

Sculpture & Water Features

The Roman naturalist and historian Pliny the Elder (AD 23–79) offers fascinating glimpses of Classical antiquity, including the townhouses and country villas of his era. Since the seminal cultures of Greece and Rome have shaped our ideas of beauty to this day, it is interesting to note how many features of traditional garden decor are rooted in the ancient city-states and empires of the Mediterranean. They include stone statuary, pillars and pedestals, obelisks, sundials, armillary spheres (once used as astronomical instruments), bas-relief wall plaques, animal sculptures, fountains, pools, and cisterns.

Pliny's description of his own Tuscan villa enumerates many of the Classical ornaments and designs that still inspire us today:

"Having passed through several winding alleys, you enter a straight walk, which breaks out into a variety of others, divided by box edges. In one place you have a little meadow; in another the box is trimmed into a thousand different forms...while here and there, little obelisks rise, intermixed with fruit trees. At the upper end is an alcove of white marble, shaded with vines, supported by four small columns of Carystian marble. Here is a triclinium [a couch for reclining at a three-sided table] out of which the water,

gushing through several little pipes, as if it were pressed out by the weight of the persons who repose upon it, falls into a stone cistern underneath, from whence it is received into a fine polished marble basin, so artfully contrived that it is always full without ever overflowing..... Corresponding to this is a fountain, which is incessantly emptying and filling; for the water, which it throws up to a great height, falling back again into it, is returned as fast as it is received, by means of two openings."

Sundial plates, with their shadow-casting gnomons, were usually mounted on a pedestal to serve as the focal point of intersecting walks or parterres in formal gardens. Most of the antique sundials inspired by the Renaissance date from the end of the eighteenth century, and many have served as templates for contemporary reproductions. As the British writer Alistair Morris observes in *Antiques from the Garden*: "[The sundial] may comprise a dial, usually of bronze, engraved with the hours and compass points together with its gnomon, and be fixed vertically to a wall or placed horizontally on a pedestal of stone, lead, cast iron or terracotta."

Gertrude Jekyll favored lead for decorative features and noted in her book *Garden Ornament* that "the general form

Opposite: This artless statue of a little girl holding a summer hat and a red peony is a delightful addition to a private garden in Jackson, California.

of the sundial base in England was the baluster, round or square in section, plain or enriched with sculptured ornament. In Scotland the more usual form was a tall shaft with obelisk top, the indication of time being given by a number of faceted forms." Antique British and European examples also include sundial plates of slate, some designed for installation at ground level, but most mounted on pedestals of marble, sandstone, Portland or Cotswold stone, and molded composition stoneware. The closely related armillary sundial had an openwork spherical form pierced by an arrow, with the hours calibrated on the sphere. (Contemporary armillary spheres serve mainly as distinctive sculptural ornaments rather than as timekeepers.) Traditionally, the sundial has been inscribed with maxims and mottoes about the passage of time, including the following:

"With my shadow moves the world."

"Silens loquor."
("Though silent, I speak.")

"Lead kindly light."

"L'heure passe, l'amitie reste."
("Time passes, friendship remains.")

"Carpe diem."
("Seize the day.")

"Hoc tuum est."
("The present is all you may claim as yours.")

Garden statuary ranges from formal to whimsical in style and is now available in a wide range of weather-resistant materials including polyresin, copper, and cast iron or aluminum with a verdigris finish. Many well-made examples are hand-painted in bright, high-contrast colors; others have a more natural, weathered

Right: *Rosedown Plantation and Gardens is a beautifully restored antebellum home and setting dating from 1835. Many of its features, including this Classical fountain, were imported from Europe to Louisiana's East Feliciana Parish by the wealthy planter who built the estate.*

Left: *Belingrath Gardens, near Mobile, Alabama, was created by architect George B. Rogers for businessman Walter D. Bellingrath during the 1930s. Its 60 acres of formal gardens were modeled on those of the stately homes in Europe.*

appearance. A random sampling of recent offerings includes a figure of Euterpe, the muse of music, finished in antique white to resemble marble; a Celtic cross of seventh-century inspiration inscribed with the Tree of Life linking heaven and earth; bas-relief wall plaques in the Classical mode, with elegant male and female profiles rendered in a rusted iron-flake finish; and gazing globes of colored glass or stainless steel mounted on graceful pedestals.

Of course, such features must be chosen and placed carefully to complement your garden style. Whether sited among shrubbery, completing a vista, or enhancing a garden room, they should be consistent with one another and with the landscape. Eighteenth-century writers enjoyed poking fun at grandiose schemes that resulted in a jumble of natural and un-natural effects like the one Alexander Pope satirized in his *Fourth Epistle* (1731):

"The suffering eye inverted nature sees,
Trees cut to statues, statues thick as trees;
With here a fountain, never to be played;
And there a summer-house, that knows
no shade."

The English garden designer Batty Langley was equally severe in his 1728 treatise *New Principles of Gardening,* in which he observed that "There is nothing adds so much to the beauty and grandeur of gardens as fine statues; and nothing more disagreeable than when wrongly placed; as Neptune on a terrace walk...or Pan, the god of sheep, in a canal or a fountain." Not many of us need to worry about canals and multilevel fountains today, but the principle of coherence remains applicable whether we are working with Greek gods or pink flamingoes.

Mushroom-shaped antique staddle stones, used for centuries as footings for granaries to protect the harvest from rodents, are now in great demand as garden ornaments. Auction houses in England sell them for high prices, and Yankee entrepreneurs have begun crafting faithful replicas combining concrete and peat to form a porous surface that promotes the growth of moss and lichens. Another legacy from the Old World is the use of weathered stone troughs, old sinks, and cisterns as planters and water features. These became very scarce in England after World War I as a result of their popularity with rock gardeners, so enterprising suppliers developed the material known as hypertufa, or moldable stone. This versatile material, composed of peat moss, sand, and cement, can be used to fashion natural-looking stepping stones, birdbaths, water basins, and a host of other attractive garden features.

Victorian-style ornaments reflect the era's idealization of nature, family life,

Below: This close-up view of a gazing ball in a Sutter Creek, California, garden shows how these spheres reflect the beauty around them.

fairy tales, and the picturesque in general. Many of those available today originated in period illustrations for children's books, or the work of early members of the Arts and Crafts movement, informed by medieval sources. Cherubic children with domestic animals are faithful to this style; so are fairylike figures holding fruit or flowers and trellises of Gothic form. Scrollwork and foliate features inspired by elaborate nineteenth-century metalwork designs are the perfect complement to the many Victorian "Painted Ladies" and landscapes that are being lovingly restored across the nation.

The serene influence of the East has become increasingly apparent in Western gardens in recent decades, as seen in the wealth of Oriental images and design principles being used by American gardeners today. Stone figurines of the Buddha, curvilinear cranes symbolizing long life and happiness, pagoda sculptures based on antique Chinese ceramics, and the playful Japanese *maneki-neko*, or beckoning cat, have all found a place in our landscapes. Replicas of exotic fan-tailed golden fish and ornamental carp are eye-catchers on a stone-flagged terrace, while their real-life counterparts are increasingly seen in pools, ponds, and other water features. Naturally, a stone lantern does not constitute a true Japanese garden, which is often the work of a lifetime. But the ambience of order and peace in these gardens has been successfully reprised by American designers, including nonprofessionals, who have made a close study of the principles underlying this ancient art form.

Animal sculptures are a natural component of garden decor. Formal estate gardens may have life-size images of seated or couchant lions at their gates. Stags, dragons, sphinxes, foxes, wolves, and bears have all figured in historic parklike landscapes, and both wild and domestic animals remain popular ornamental features of less imposing form. Stone turtles, terra-cotta rabbits, and folk-art frogs add charm to the garden, and a realistic sleeping cat appears entirely at home in a flowerbed (and poses no threat to the birds you may wish to attract). In fact, birds are perhaps the most popular subjects of garden art. Who hasn't seen a front yard cheered by a stoneware goose, perhaps sporting a colorful child's bonnet à la Beatrice Potter? Realistic ducks, swans, cranes, and herons are used to striking effect around water features, and popular songbirds could have a chapter to themselves, especially since the birdbath is a nearly ubiquitous ornament that often includes an avian sculpture. It was not always so. In earlier times, most householders were concerned about getting *rid* of the birds that might raid their berries and grains. Not until the nature-loving late nineteenth century did ornamental birdbaths gain a foothold in the garden.

An early twentieth-century catalogue from Great Britain illustrates a number of stone and composition birdbaths, ranging from shallow bowls on Classical pedestals to a shell-like saucer based on a squirrel-shaped support. A footed urn only 10 inches high was advertised as a "lawn bird bath" (and birds do, in fact, seek bath and drinking water at ground level). Some of the baths illustrated had prayers or poetry inscribed on their bases, including the famous line from Coleridge, "He prayeth best who loveth best all things both great and small." Today we have birdbaths in many other styles, from

formal to playful, freestanding to hanging or deck-mounted. A few simple precautions will make them an asset to both birds and landscape. These include siting them in an open area where marauding housecats can't conceal themselves, and keeping the water fresh and clean. A sunny location is best, to discourage the breeding of mosquitos and algae formation. Low-growing plants in front and

Above: The Baroque Moses Fountain, rimmed by geraniums, adorns the Munsterplatz in Bern, Switzerland.

taller plants behind the bath frame it attractively during the summer months, and a number of solar heaters and de-icers are now available to help nonmigratory songbirds survive the winter, when drinking water freezes.

Surveys indicate that fountains, pools, and water gardens are among the most-desired decorative elements for the garden, not only in the United States, but worldwide. Through history, they have served to recall the Garden of Eden, with its life-giving river that divided to form streams that flowed to the four directions. Perhaps you are fortunate enough to have a natural stream running through your property that can be enhanced by suitable plantings, or graded with boulders

to form small waterfalls. If not, garden suppliers have devised innumerable ways to install ornamental pools and ponds made of concrete, galvanized steel, fiberglass, butyl-rubber sheeting, and various plastics. Both streams and ponds can be bridged by a simple arched footbridge of wooden planks, or by a more ornate bridge in any suitable style, now widely available in different price ranges. You may prefer to design your own, perhaps in the geometric Chippendale style, or a more rustic creation combining split logs and a wooden railing.

Many would-be water gardeners content themselves with a half-barrel that will support several aquatic plants, including a waterlily, in submerged containers sunk

Below: A triple-tiered fountain rises from an overflowing bowl at the Mediterranean-style Viscaya Pavilion and Gardens in Sacramento, California.

at different levels. Others experiment with concrete pools in various shapes and sizes, for which authorities recommend the proportions of one part Portland cement, two parts sand, and three parts gravel. Such a pool should be poured without seams—first the floor, then the walls, before the floor hardens. The labor involved is rewarded by a pool that is both strong and watertight. The edges can be finished in any suitable material, or concealed by rocks to provide a natural look.

Multilevel pools with a waterfall between them are another option. Many gardeners are doing the excavating themselves and installing appropriate lining materials and a pump to recirculate the water. The pool will then support both plant life and fish, adding a new dimension to the landscape. It can be further enhanced by sprays and jets of water from submersible nozzles, or by floating solar fountains.

Freestanding or wall-hung fountains like those used for centuries in Spanish courtyards also provide the soothing, cooling sound of running water. Decorative rockwork or tilework around such water features gives them even greater presence. For the small city garden, there are tabletop-size fountains that can be tucked in among foliage or flowering plants: Japanese-style bowls filled with smooth river rocks washed by recirculating water, and multilevel copper fountains in which the water cascades from one tier to another. A round reflecting pool, perhaps with a raised edge, is an ideal setting for a sculptural fountain that fills the air with a delicate intersecting spray. Seashells, cherubs, and nymphs may ornament a Renaissance-style fountain in the formal garden, while an old millstone edged by smooth rocks that conceal a catch basin

makes an ideal accent with a foot-high fountain surging up through its center.

The possibilities are endless, as suggested by Doug Stewart in the article "Fountains: Splash and Spectacle" (*Smithsonian*, May 1998 issue). Here he describes the first major exhibition on fountain design through history, mounted by the Smithsonian's Cooper-Hewitt National Design Museum in New York City that year. As he observes: "Fountains are perhaps the most mercurial of all art forms. Since the Renaissance and before, they've teased the imaginations of artists while testing the know-how of engineers. Water can't be shaped with a chisel or a mold, but in the hands of a fountain designer it can be coaxed into an endless number of forms: geysers, cascades, trickles, tubes, moving sheets, clouds of spray, even ice and steam. Small wonder that fountains affect us in such dramatically different ways."

Above: An elegant crested bird in topiary form overlooks a formal garden flanked by an enclosed walkway with massive Gothic windows.

Topiary Takes Flight *Opposite*
This living sculpture of an eagle was patiently crafted for the formal gardens at Bayou Bend in Houston, Texas. Massed lavender-hued azaleas fill the border behind it.

A Woven Sculpture *Below*
This cone of twigs, surrounded by a bed of lavender, makes a striking natural accent at Amador Flower Farm in Plymouth, California.

The Orient Rising

A five-tiered pagoda marks the landscape receding behind it in the Japanese Garden at Washington Park in Portland, Oregon (below). On the opposite page is a weathered sculpture of an Asian elephant "grazing" on the foliage of plants around its base in Tacoma, Washington's, Lakewold Garden.

Wreathed in Greenery *Previous pages*

A Classical sculpture of a beautiful woman (page 138) wears a floral crown echoed by the foliage that drapes so naturally around her. The childlike angel (page 139), a symbol of protection and spiritual guidance, is adorned with tendrils of English ivy.

A Study in Bronze *Below*

The powerful sculpture *Lioness and Cub,* by Hope Wandell, is perfectly sited on slabs of shelving rock in Brookgreen Gardens, South Carolina.

Diana of the Chase *Opposite*

Grace animates this beautiful bronze sculpture of the goddess Diana (Artemis), poised on a sphere with one of her hunting dogs eager to begin the chase. Sculpted by Anna Hyatt Huntington in 1922, this noble sculpture now ornaments Brookgreen Gardens.

Elizabethan Splendor *Overleaf*

This sunken garden with balustraded pool and fountain surrounded by edged beds marks the site of the first unsuccessful attempt by English colonists to settle in the New World at Roanoke Island, North Carolina, in 1585. The outdoor drama *The Lost Colony* is enacted in nearby Manteo every year.

Under the Wolf Tree   *Page 144*
The venerable "Wolf Tree" presides over the sculptures and plantings that combine to form a secluded shade garden with an oriental ambience at Lakewood Garden in Tacoma, Washington.

A Vessel of Abundance   *Page 145*
A Classical nymph pours a symbolic stream, representing the water of life that sustains the Earth, from her urn in the herb garden of California's Amador Farm, surrounded by the stately forms of ripening artichokes, with their spreading, saw-toothed leaves.

Rosedown: A World Apart   *Above and opposite*
Shown above is a close view of the Renaissance fountain at Rosedown Plantation, Louisiana, with the encircling parterre that replicates the rounded pool. Entwined dolphins in the plantation's octagonal pool (opposite) support a cherub seated in a shell and gazing toward the pagoda-roofed gazebo.

Afton Villa's Formal Garden   *Overleaf*
Not far from Rosedown is Afton Villa, a mansion with another breathtaking formal garden restored to its original beauty in St. Francisville, Louisiana.

A Humorous Touch *Previous page*
This brightly painted Victorian-style image of a boy
holding up his wet boot brings a smile to visitors at the
Hershey Gardens in Hershey, Pennsylvania.

An Age-old Water Source *Below*
The stone basin below, fed by a bamboo pipe hinged on
a tripod, is a traditional Japanese drinking fountain in
the Kinkakuji Garden at Kyoto.

A Japanese Cistern *Opposite*
The deep stone trough opposite, with its long-handled
drinking cups resting on a framework of bamboo, is fed
by an underground spring at the Shinto shrine (Katsuga
Taisha) in Nara, Japan.

Right at Home

This lifelike rabbit is a pleasing addition to a colorful naturalistic flower bed at Farmers Branch Historic Park near Dallas, Texas. Note the tulips emerging after the spring showing of the delicate pansies, which thrive on chilly weather.

Finishing Touch *Overleaf*

A naturalistic four-part masonry fountain is enhanced by the basin at the lowest level. Multilevel water features provide a particularly welcome and refreshing addition to gardens enjoyed by people with compromised eyesight.

Gator-Aid *Below*

Nestled in a sea of tall camouflage grass, the life-sized— and lifelike—alligator below gives visitors a double-take when they stop in at the homely Cabin Restaurant near Baton Rouge, Louisiana.

Centerpiece *Page 155*

A simple birdbath in a thick, tapered base is the focal point of a planted terrace of random paving ringed by exuberant borders in a Seattle, Washington, garden.

Lavishly Adorned *Pages 156-57*

The luxuriant growth of this Savannah, Georgia, garden is complemented by the central fountain, well-placed sculpture, and potted plants. The symmetrical edging of wood chips is in keeping with the garden's style, which blends naturalistic and formal elements.

Realism in Garden Art *Opposite*

The bronze sculpture of a seated boy on a cypress stump is entitled *Long, Long Thoughts*. This pensive work was created by Charles Parks in 1922 and ornaments South Carolina's Brookgreen Gardens.

The Rose Garden at Rosedown *Below*

Enclosed by a curving boxwood parterre, the plantation's acclaimed rose garden is visible beyond the circular fountain in the foreground.

Lily of the Day *Page 160*

An angel birdbath comes to life with the addition of a glowing Ruby Claret day lily at Amador Flower Farm in Plymouth, California. Cut blooms are sadly short-lived, but this is a clever use for broken-stemmed flowers.

Ornamental Perfection *Page 161*

A Renaissance-style sundial with a stylized bird becomes even more memorable surrounded by delicate white cosmos and a single peerless rose.

In the Spanish Style *Above*
A masonry fountain and pebbled terrace showcase the
plaza garden at California's Carmel Mission Basilica.

Shimmering Colors *Page 162-63*
Tulips bloom within the boxwood maze at Afton Villa's
gardens in St. Francisville, Louisiana.

Showing Fall Colors *Below*

A romantic Victorian-style fountain of a young couple cast in white composition stone is an ideal complement to the riotous colors of fall chrysanthemums at Bill's Apple Farm in Camino, California.

Nineteenth-century Treasure *Below*

This well-worn sculpture of a boy reclining on a pedestal was chosen for Rosedown Plantation by the wealthy planter who canvassed Europe and the United States to ornament his gardens.

Stone on Stone *Above*

A view of the trellised tea house at Tacoma's Lakewold Garden, with its carved pedestals, Classical urns, and planted base for the graceful sculpture that is seen also in a close-up detail on page 138.

The Endless Summer *Overleaf*

Oriental lilies sound a jubilant note in this delightful and vibrantly colorful cottage garden in historic Charlottetown, Prince Edward Island.

Thrusting Toward the Sky *Page 169*

An elegant armillary sphere encompasses the beds and borders around it and leads the eye upward toward more distant vistas.

The Play of Waters *Below*

The elegant latticework gazebo at Rosedown is enhanced by a pair of pedestaled fountains that fling their delicate sprays upward to cool the sultry Louisiana summer air.

Oasis *Opposite*

A dreamlike crystalline pool fed by a cooling natural spring invites contemplation at Tacoma's serene and beautiful Lakewold Garden.

The Mysterious East *Opposite*

The serene Moss Garden is on the grounds of Japan's Kinkakuji Temple in Kyoto. Carefully designed, every natural and manmade feature of such a garden has its own spiritual significance.

A World-Renowned Dutch Garden *Below*

The Keukenhof Flower Gardens in the Netherlands are a magnet for visitors when the tulips are in bloom around the lakeside. The tulip grows so prolifically in this country that it has become a national emblem.

Light and Shadow *Overleaf*

This graceful seated figure adorns the gardens of time-honored Middletown Place Plantation, near Charleston, South Carolina (1755). The property is now an estate museum with the nation's oldest landscaped gardens.

Guardian Cherubs *Page 175*

Friendly cherubs oversee the luxuriant gardens at the Burn (1835) along the famous Natchez Trace in Mississippi, where some of the nation's most imposing plantations have been preserved and restored.

Shelters & Sanctuaries

Perhaps the most delightful aspect of such open-air garden structures as gazebos, pergolas, and arbors is that they provide a sense of shelter from the elements while allowing us to remain out of doors, enjoying the fresh air despite a hot summer sun or a sudden shower. Somehow, they partake of the feeling evoked by the children's phrase "a secret hideout." The same feeling is summoned up by the sight of a treehouse, or a playhouse in a grove where the sun slants through the leaves to give the scene a quality of enchantment. Thomas Wolfe admonished us in his moving novel of 1940 that "You can't go home again," but the glimpse of a distant pavilion, or the inviting aspect of a flower-laden pergola that leads the eye beyond what it can see, seem to suggest that you can recapture that feeling of homecoming in such moments.

History offers us many examples of pleasing garden structures, from the Roman orator Cicero's beloved Tuscan and Formian villas to artist Claude Monet's living masterpiece at Giverny, France, immortalized by his paintings. The remains of extensive terraced gardens with cooling arcades and arbors were discovered during the nineteenth-century excavations at Pompeii, and contemporary accounts of Roman villas describe gardens encircled by a carriage drive and "a shady walk of vines, soft and tender even to the naked feet." At Pliny the Younger's Laurentine estate, there was a freestanding portico "having windows on one side looking to the sea, on the other to the garden."

During the Renaissance era, similar Classical features were created for the grounds of wealthy noblemen, primarily in stone. Then England's growing class of landed gentry began to embellish their properties with grottos, pavilions, and ha-has—ornamental fences set into sloping ground to prevent livestock from straying into the landscape. When such structures were made of wood, they tended to collapse after a few seasons. Nineteenth-century advances in technology made it possible to build attractive and durable garden structures in iron and wirework as well as more traditional materials. Gazebos and "rose temples" were produced in a variety of designs, including the popular octagonal form with a domed, cone-shaped, or pagoda-style roofline. Rambling plants were trained over the supports to form bowers furnished with benches and tables, where people could dine or simply relax in the shade.

These shelters were usually crowned by a finial or an orb and ornamented with delicate scrollwork—spiral-shaped,

Opposite: The airy latticework gazebo at Rosedown, crowned by a handsome finial, is raised slightly above ground level on a masonry footing to prevent the wood from deteriorating in Louisiana's hot, damp climate.

Below: This delightful dovecote, or pigeon house, built to hold twenty pairs of birds, was supported on a strong 15-foot-high framework to keep the occupants safe from predators (c.1910).

The traditional Japanese garden is an exemplar of the melding of garden structures and landscape features into a seamless whole. We can profit by its principles even if we do not garden in this style. The essence of Japanese gardening (which drew heavily upon Chinese practice in its evolution) is to replicate the natural landscape in miniature in a highly symbolic way. There is an underlying system of allusions and symbols that convey meaning to visitors imbued with this tradition. However small, the true Japanese garden comprises a complex of scenes that evoke natural features—mountains and valleys, rivers and lakes. Fine white gravel raked into fluid patterns symbolizes the stream of life, and carefully selected stones are arranged to create a microcosmic mountain range, in which each stone has spiritual significance.

The path of stepping stones from the *chuman* (entry arch) to the tea house signifies the passage to illumination. The traditional bamboo water pipe runs through a thicker length of bamboo with a hollowed-out chamber: as the water flows out, the pipe falls back upon a rock with a sharp clacking sound. (This water feature was originally designed to frighten wild boar or deer away from the crops.) The tea house, or pergola, may be suggested by a latticework or bamboo canopy over a paved area that faces the innermost part of the garden, or it may be a self-contained structure with sliding panels that open it to the outdoors. Traditional plantings include various forms of the Japanese maple, including *Acer palmatum*, clipped evergreen trees and shrubs, ferns, moss, and flowering shrubs like the azalea. The stepping stones are placed with studied irregularity to lead the visitor through the garden, where boulders and stone lanterns highlight various features. Since this art form was introduced from the Far East, its timeless serenity and order have had a major influence on Western thinking about garden design.

Not to be overlooked is the ancient craft of pleaching, which yields a living structure that becomes self-reinforcing over time. It was originally developed by farmers to make their hedges more secure by bending the trunks and branches of young trees and weaving them together to form architectural shapes. Examples can be seen in Colonial Williamsburg,

Virginia, where this form of garden art was imported from England, and in many private gardens where it is enjoying a revival. The demand for arbors and follies on English estates brought pleaching from the farm to the parklike grounds of wealthy patrons. Pleached structures proved far more durable than those made of nonliving wood, which often succumbed to rot or the elements after a few seasons. In the case of arbors, the cumulative weight of vigorously growing vines like wisteria often brought them down.

European gardeners still form hedges and structures by pleaching, and if one has the patience to wait for results, the process is simple. Young trees are planted in the configuration desired—say, opposite one another to form a tunnel—and pruned to the desired height before the pliant new shoots are tied together at the top to form an arch. Outward-facing branches are pruned away, and side branches on the inner walls are tied back to leave a clear path. Suckers are removed as they appear, and desirable new shoots are bent and tied in place.

The technique for making a formal pleached hedge as a backdrop for other plantings is even simpler. You can use slow-growing specimens like the trees favored by English gardeners, including beech, holly, hornbeam, linden, and yew, or faster-growing species like birch, sycamore, and willow. In either case, the saplings should be planted four to five feet apart and trained to a single stem. The lower part of the trunk should be kept free of branches, and the upper branches pruned to encourage lateral (sideways) growth. After a few seasons, a dense network of branches and twigs will extend between the trees. Once they have

reached the desired height and width, you can then shear the densely leaved top and sides to produce a geometric outline.

Burgeoning awareness of the need for conservation and ecological balance has produced many new types of shelter and sanctuary for the creatures who share our living space. Birdhouses and feeders are being used more and more widely, and they come in a wide array of decorative designs and weatherproof materials. Craftspeople are remastering the art of fashioning birdhouses from clay, wood, and dried gourds to encourage songbirds to nest in their yards, just as farmers once cut swallow holes in the gables of their barns to invite these helpful insect-eaters to roost there. Dovecotes, which originally served the practical purpose of raising birds for the table, are now built to attract and protect their tenants while adding architectural interest to the garden.

Scientific studies have increased our knowledge of the needs of various species, resulting in purpose-built shelters congenial to robins, goldfinches, chickadees,

Above: Scalloped eaves and a tiny portico invite immediate occupancy of this pedestal bird cottage in a Canadian garden.

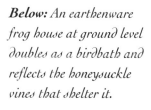
and other birds. A survey of current offerings includes a hanging earthenware wren house with a hammered-copper roof and a tiny entry hole; a post-mounted, Newport-style wooden nesting house capped by a ball finial; a hand-painted *chinoiserie* house made of terra cotta; and a pole-mounted, twelve-room "apartment house" for attracting gregarious purple martins. Special bluebird nesting boxes of white pine, with predator-proof openings and raised wire-mesh flooring for ventilation, have been instrumental in helping both Eastern and Western bluebird populations to recover from a long decline. Mounted in series on fences or trees as "bluebird trails," they will promote a garden filled with colorful spring and summer activity. And cozy English roosting pockets of woven jute provide life-giving shelter for nonmigratory birds that winter over in cold climates.

Bird feeders, too, have benefited from growing knowledge about the foods preferred by various species. Post-mounted feeders with gazebo-style roofs are useful

ornaments that attract seed-eaters while protecting both them and their food from the elements. Colorful tube feeders for nectar-seeking hummingbirds can be hung from the eaves and filled with a sugar-water solution irresistible to these tiny jewel-like creatures, whom John James Audubon described as "fragments of the rainbow." Woodpeckers will visit suet feeders, especially those that resemble tree trunks and open outward for refilling. And for bird-lovers who want to distract the ingenious squirrel from their feeders, a number of diversions are being offered, from two-pound blocks of mixed seed for feeding at ground level to tree-mounted platforms with spokes to hold dried corn cobs. Squirrels, after all, have to eat too.

Many a suburban backyard has been redesigned to bring back birds and wildlife to populous areas in which their habitats were shrinking. The focal point of such a yard might be the replica of a Dutch hay barrack, which consists of a pyramidal roof that can be raised or lowered on four rough-hewn timber uprights. It would serve as a rustic gazebo surrounded by a wildflower meadow that attracts birds, butterflies, and bees. Phlox, bee balm, hollyhocks, and liatris are cultivated plants that serve this purpose too.

A pond will bring both frogs and larger birds to the yard and can be planted with such hardy species as water lilies, cattails, and pickerelweed. Since toads are prodigious insect eaters, some garden-supply firms are now offering terra-cotta "toad houses" shaped like inverted bowls with a small opening at ground level. Other nature-loving shelters include butterfly houses of red cedar and other weather-resistant woods that can be filled with bark to encourage angelwings, tortoise-

Below: An earthenware frog house at ground level doubles as a birdbath and reflects the honeysuckle vines that shelter it.

shells, and fritillaries to move in. Similarly constructed hibernation boxes provide multiple small openings that simulate the crevices in which caterpillars build cocoons, providing protection from cold weather and predators. Ladybugs are being catered to with slotted and hinged boxes painted in attractive colors and mounted on a tree or fence post. These long-time favorites of both children and gardeners eat several times their weight in insect pests every day, including aphids, whiteflies, spider mites, and mealybugs.

The old-fashioned bee skeps — dome-shaped inverted baskets woven of reeds and rushes — have become popular garden ornaments, but honeybees should not be encouraged to nest in them, since their honey cannot be harvested without destroying the colony. Instead, cover the entry holes with fine screening, and if you wish to keep bees for the pollination of fruit trees and other plants, or simply to offer them shelter, provide a modern beehive with movable frames located some distance from the house or the areas where children may play. Otherwise, the colony's guard bees may emerge and sting those who come too close to the hive. Since honeybee populations are suffering from mite infestations, such shelters promote conservation, even if you do not wish to harvest the honey.

Organic gardening, without the use of chemical pesticides and fertilizers, has made great strides in the last several decades and is virtually essential to maintaining a wildlife-friendly garden. We have come to realize that many pesticides kill or harm birds and butterfly larvae directly, while others kill or contaminate insects and other creatures that birds eat. With this in mind, many experts encourage

shrinking the areas given over to turf, which is high-maintenance and provides little in the way of food, and enlarging planting beds with multilayered trees, shrubs, and flowers that provide year-round sources of food and shelter while enhancing the look of your property. These include evergreens like pines and upright juniper, with their dense needles that provide protected roosting sites; the American cranberry bush and winterberry holly, which bear bright-red berries that beautify the landscape under snow; and grapevines or other climbing plants like honeysuckle, trumpet vine, and hyacinth bean, which Thomas Jefferson grew at Monticello. Instead of fencing, consider hedges of elderberry, dogwood, and shrubby serviceberry. These techniques will pay natural dividends, not least in the form of overwintering woodpeckers, chickadees, nuthatches, and cardinals to brighten Northern gardens that are renewing their strength for the season to come.

Above: *Generous plantings enhance this informal outdoor room at a country garden on Prince Edward Island.*

Treehouse Writ Small *Page 186*

This rustic cabin-style birdhouse is the focal point of a colorful vignette that includes blooming iris encircling a fir tree on Vashon Island, Washington.

Ingenuity at Work *Opposite and below*

Inventiveness knows no bounds when it comes to crafting shelters like the gable-roofed cowboy boot opposite and the dollhouselike confection below, complete with its appliquéd figures and plantings.

Architectural Fantasy *Page 187*

These stump-mounted birdhouses, incorporating twigs and shingles, vines and moss, resemble the unique organic creations of the Spanish architect Antonio Gaudi. They were photographed at Fasmer's, in Pine Grove, California.

Split-rail Residence *Pages 188-89*

A tiny American flag marks this folk-art birdhouse mounted on a split-rail fence at the border of a colorful woodland in Bureau County, Illinois.

Greeting the Day *Opposite*
This bountifully planted terrace, with its classic white wicker furnishings, is a delightful *al fresco* breakfast nook at the Korab residence in Troy, Michigan.

Picturesque Ruins *Below*
Tumbledown brickwork at Louisiana's Afton Villa has been artfully incorporated into this corner garden on the grounds of the old plantation.

A Well-placed Pavilion *Opposite*

Fall colors highlight this latticework gazebo nestled among the trees of Lake Marie Garden in Amador County, California.

Frontier-style Shelter *Below*

The Swedish-style log cabin below is a relic of pioneer settlement preserved in a grove at Zilker Botanical Park in Austin, Texas.

Oriental Effects *Overleaf*

The pagoda-roofed gazebo at water's edge has its counterpoint in the white footbridge that spans the lake at Monmouth Garden in Natchez, Mississippi, built during the 1820s by John A. Quitman.

Forecourt and Pergola *Above*
A concrete path follows the curve of the low stone wall leading to a stepped pergola in this attractive approach to a secluded house in California.

Clouds of Glory *Opposite*
Brilliant rhododendrons light up the garden of the Heirloom Bed and Breakfast in Ione, California, where guests can enjoy a quiet retreat in this sheltered gazebo.

Splendor in the Valley *Overleaf*
The beautiful Byodo-in Temple, on the island of Oahu, Hawaii, is part of the complex called the Valley of the Temples, which reflects the state's Polynesian and Pacific cultural heritage.

At the Golden Gate *Opposite*

The elegant multitiered pagodas in the Japanese Tea Garden in San Francisco's Golden Gate Park bear witness to the contribution of California's immigrants from the Far East.

Symmetry Reigns *Below*

A wide brick walkway flanked by box-edged parterres and topiary leads to the latticed Tea House in this elegant formal garden.

Hispanic Heritage *Overleaf*

This tile-roofed patio alcove at the historic Carmel Mission in Carmel, California, ornamented with ferns and flowers, is a shrine to the Virgin Mary and the Child Jesus. The stucco facing on the masonry walls has partly worn away.

Outdoor Room with a View *Above*
The highly placed gazebo above commands the grounds of an impressive Natchez, Mississippi, estate house on what is known as the Natchez Pilgrimage.

Rosedown Plantation *Right*
The azalea garden at Rosedown opens to a view of the plantation's venerable trees and the graceful gazebo that is the focal point of several sweeping vistas.

An Informal Affair *Opposite*

This generously sized pavilion with brick steps leading down to an outdoor dining area is a rural retreat for its owners in Plymouth, California.

A Handsome Memorial *Below*

The imposing plaza below, in Houston, Texas, with its ornamental ironwork and stone columns and piers, is part of a public garden dedicated to survivors of cancer.

A Spanish Baroque Shrine *Overleaf*

This patio enclave in California bears a tilework image of Our Lady of Mount Carmel in an ornate frame surmounted by a metal plaque depicting the cross of Christ wreathed in the crown of thorns.

N. S. DO CARMO

An Unusual Rectangular Shelter *Above*
A raised gazebo in the Victorian style overlooks a circular walk and island bed ringed by summer flowers
and graceful wisteria in this grand Southern garden.

Pacific Island Garden *Below*
The traditional grass shelter below, beautified by a pink-flowered hibiscus, stands in the Polynesian Cultural Center at Laii, on Oahu.

Pueblo-style Outdoor Room *Opposite*
The earth-colored brick and warm tones and organic shapes of the adobe walls and inbuilt seating make the patio a relaxing retreat at this New Mexico home.

Southwestern Oasis *Above*
Desert rubblestone frames this refreshing pool at architect Frank Lloyd Wright's Taliesin West (1937) in Scottsdale, Arizona.

In Harmony with Nature *Overleaf*
This classical structure of timber, tile, and masonry is integral with its setting in the Japanese Garden at Portland's Washington Park.

Folk Art & Found Objects

To personalize your garden, folk art and found objects including old tools, wagon wheels, weathervanes, and memorabilia of family trips and special events offer a host of possibilities. Whether whimsical, useful, or both, they add the touches that make the garden uniquely your own.

The toy-size action figures known as whirligigs—popular garden ornaments at the turn of the twentieth century—are enjoying a nationwide revival, with many home craftsmen designing and making their own. These wooden, wind-powered, painted figures include a small propeller to catch the breeze and can be mounted on poles or fences to bring movement and a sense of fun to the informal garden. Based on the pinwheel principle, they are adapted from American folk-art weathervanes originally whittled from elm or birch, or other native woods. Modern adaptations have ball-bearing centers that twirl the arms, legs, or wings of the brightly painted figures—mallards, bluebirds, frogs, angels, Holstein cows, cats, and more. They whirl on their perches with every change in the wind direction and serve to frighten away common garden pests without the use of chemicals. Handmade examples along regional country roads include a Nevada

miner wielding his pick, a farmer milking his cow, and a logger sawing at a stump.

Traditional rooftop weathervanes are another collectible form of folk art that is now appreciated more for its ornamental than its practical value. Early American weathervanes were carved from wood or forged in blacksmiths' shops and forge barns—special tool houses and "repair shops" in which farmers mended their implements and created new tools, including the weathervane. Formed in the shape of arrows, pointing hands, horses, and roosters (which accounts for the name "weathercock"), these devices were indispensable to the farmer, who could discern from the direction in which the wind was blowing whether to expect fair weather for planting or a sudden storm that necessitated getting the crops in without delay.

As animal husbandry became more widespread, cows and pigs became familiar figures on the rooftop or cupola. During the later decades of the nineteenth century, both weathervanes and elaborate cupolas for rooftop ventilation of barns could be ordered from farm-supply catalogues. Horses and cows were most in demand, but seaside dwellers might display a fish or a whale. These original weathervanes are now valuable antiques, but faithful reproductions in weather-

Opposite: Preparing for the annual Symphony of Daffodils at the Kautz Ironstone Winery in Murphys, California. Floral and seasonal banners have become popular outdoor accents.

old watering cans filled with fresh flowers, and hand-crafted birdhouses and feeders in the form of log cabins, village churches, and thatched-roof cottages. An old bicycle tire nailed to the top of a post will soon be wreathed in clematis or morning-glory vines if you run lengths of twine from the base to the rim of the wheel. Mailbox posts, too, become an attractive feature when underplanted with colorful annuals or wreathed in vines.

Wheelbarrows are popular garden ornaments that can be filled with potted plants, or even made into small, portable rock gardens. Many gardeners are enthusiastic rock collectors, and your choice finds in nearby streams and woods could become the basis for an interesting decorative feature of this kind. Thrifty craftsmen have found that old gas grills can be recycled into handy potting stations by removing the inner workings and filling them with soil, then adding hooks for tools on either side. Half-barrels make sturdy informal planters and can also be waterproofed to serve as small water gardens during the summer months. And replicas of the old-fashioned prairie windmill are being made in various sizes to serve as vertical accents and plant supports. The blades spin freely in response to the slightest breeze, recalling the angular structures that powered the Great Plains for decades.

Paint can do wonders in transforming a drab liability into an asset. A weathered garden shed, for example, can become a

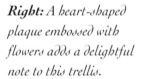

Right: A heart-shaped plaque embossed with flowers adds a delightful note to this trellis.

mural when painted with a folk-art land-scape, or decorated with cast-off tools spray-painted in bright primary colors and nailed on in a random pattern. The same homely structure can serve as a can-vas for feed sacks, flower pots, painted family pets, or any other subject that pleases you, much as old barns were dec-orated with advertisements and pictures of the farm animals raised there.

Don't be afraid to experiment with breaking the rules that tell us to "Keep it simple" and "Stick to a single theme." Delightful effects can be created by a col-lection of garden gnomes placed at vari-ous heights all over a colorful cottage garden, or use eye-catching "peekers" like an amusing giraffe's head emerging from the shrubbery. Your local nursery or gar-den shop will have good ideas, and so will you. If you like the pure kitsch effect of a whitewashed burro pulling a flower cart, go for it. Garden designer Marianne Binetti, the author of *Shortcuts for Accenting Your Garden*, had an amusing answer for a correspondent who wrote in to complain: "How do I tell my neighbors that their plastic geese and raccoons are tacky?" She responded that "It seems to me you have more of a problem than your neighbor does. Let them adorn their property as they want, and you decorate your garden the way you prefer. Learn to enjoy the sense of fun and frolic that your neighbors are so generously sharing with the world. And be thankful those aren't real geese in his front yard—large fowl can be very noisy."

Handmade edgings made of river cane or willow branches have a long history in garden decor. English gardeners have wattled borders out of willow for gener-ations, and pliable plant materials native to your region will blend naturally with

their surroundings. American gardeners have used cattail stems, dogwood, beech, and river cane to construct low, woven edgings around flower and vegetable beds, with sturdy hardwood stakes supporting the weaving. The effect is that of a large basket that contains the plant materials. Cane or bamboo teepees for climbing plants provide a rustic vertical dimension to wattled beds of this type. Similar woven edgings can be used along pathways in country and woodland-style gardens. The natural materials will not last indefinitely, but they are easily renewed.

Above: *The classic tale of* Alice in Wonderland *may have inspired this humorous playing-card figure high in the rafters of a timber pergola.*

Above: *An old farm implement embedded in a wildflower meadow filled with phlox enhances this spacious Midwestern vista.*

slovenly, deficient in the expression of art, and indicative of unrefined ways."

Should you be fortunate enough to have a small spring on your property, you might create a wishing well that has the advantage of supplying cool water, unlike the artificial varieties that are often purchased as ornaments. Such a well should be very shallow, so as not to present a danger to children or animals—no more than two or three feet deep. An underground channel leading away from the well will keep the water clear, but for drinking purposes, it must be tested for purity. Many books on water features and garden ornament provide detailed instructions on the lining, walls, and timber uprights and roof for a working well. Old country properties and former farms often have a picturesque feature of this kind that can be restored, or even a stone springhouse once used to store milk, butter, and other perishables before the advent of refrigeration.

Among the most appropriate found objects for the informal garden are old tools and farm implements. Architectural photographer Balthazar Korab, many of whose pictures appear in these pages, purchased an old farm on four acres in Troy, Michigan, with his wife, Monica, in the late 1950s. In 1990 horticultural writer Ogden Tanner visited the Korabs to write about the garden they had created there for *Horticulture* magazine ("A Photographer's Focus," August issue). Mr. Tanner was struck by the Korabs' artistic use of natural and manmade features to transform their original "run-down farmland" into a garden that "may not be typically Midwestern, but in many ways it is even more American: eclectic yet original, intensely personal, a landscape of the mind's eye.

More durable edgings of clay tile, with braided, arched, or scalloped tops, were preferred by Victorian gardeners and are enjoying a revival today. Fortunately, we are not confined by the strictures laid down by Edward Kemp, in his decisive Victorian way, in the book *Landscape Gardening* (1850): "[Edgings] should be quite smooth, thoroughly flat along the margins, and have some of their width at least, precisely on the same level at both sides and very well defined, though not more than half an inch above the level of the side of the walk....Walks that are not carefully formed in accordance with these conditions will appear more or less

"Massive timbers from a demolished barn were buried upright on a central earth mound, which was shaped by a backhoe to suggest the hills of Italy. Dubbed 'Baloney' after the towers of Bologna, the timbers long framed a view from the Korabs' bedroom window, where they could be appreciated first thing in the morning and again at night. The tallest eventually fell down and was promptly incorporated, where it lay, into another composition. The old farmers' lilacs are still there, now celebrated as a sculptural group, with branches pruned upward to reveal gracefully twisting trunks. The big silver maples are there, too; a hollow in one is occupied by a raccoon family that on summer evenings is sometimes seen peering comically at guests on the terrace below. Part of the property is kept in meadow, with clumps of bright poppies planted to frame the wheels of an old horse-drawn farm machine."

In the decade since this article was written, this Michigan garden has evolved still further with the vicissitudes of nature that we all experience from season to season, and with the owners' passion for collecting, experimenting, forming, and re-forming the place they have made their own. Few pastimes can compare with the satisfaction offered by creating an environment that reflects one's interests, ideas, and memories in living, ever-changing form. As Mr. Korab has observed from an artist's standpoint (and every garden-maker is an artist at heart): "A garden is not a product, it's a process."

Left: An architectural sculpture group by Balthazar Korab combines curvilinear unbarked tree rounds with an irregular stepped form rising toward the living trees around it.

Western-style Ornament

Old hydraulic mining equipment (below) has been incorporated into the extensive gardens of the Kautz Ironstone Winery—a reminder of California's glory days as a rich source of gold. On the opposite page is an iron gate that opens to the Kennedy barn in Volcano, California, studded with horseshoes, spurs, bits, and other riding paraphernalia.

For the Fun of It *Opposite and below*
Colorful garden gnomes (opposite) of all shapes and
sizes, frolicking among white-painted rock edging,
columns, and statuary, make this terraced garden a fan-
tasy carnival. Below, lavishly decorated for Easter, a
Sutter Creek, California, home greets spring with bound-
less enthusiasm.

A Garden Wish Come True *Opposite*

A Victorian-style wishing well of stoneware and lacy wrought-ironwork centers the formal herb garden on the opposite page. Note how the antique, moss-grown brick wall blends with the well and the stoneware basket of fruits and flowers at the entryway.

Decorative Ceramic Tilework *Below*

The curving stairway below features hand-painted ceramic tiles decorated in traditional Hispano-Moorish geometric and floral patterns. Spanish-influenced architecture and decorative garden features are seen widely in Florida, California, and the desert Southwest.

Folk Artistry *Below*
Both ornamental and useful, this metal fence keeps livestock from straying from the farmyard at the Kennedy ranch in Volcano, California. Its horseshoes and wagon-wheel motif throw a shadow on the stone-banked courtyard.

A Formidable Watcher *Opposite*
The rugged chain-saw carving of a Bigfoot, or Sasquatch, might well startle visitors to the garden-decor shop called Bigfoot Burl in Redwoods, California.

Pioneer Style *Below*

The old Conestoga wagonbed below, its traveling days
long over, combines harmoniously with other relics of
the Western frontier at a rough-hewn log cabin in
Sonoma, California.

Still Tolling *Above*

A bell once used to summon ranch hands (above) now announces visitors to the Broll Mountain Vineyards in California's Calaveras County.

Terrace Decor *Overleaf*

Antique winemaking equipment is the perfect comple- ment to colorful plantings in half-barrels and earthen- ware containers on the terrace outside the Kautz Ironstone Winery.

Knee-deep in Spring Flowers *Left*

Most rabbits are unwelcome visitors to the garden, but the colorful bunnies at left are a charming addition to this colorful flowerbed at Faught's Tulip Garden in Lockeford, California.

Tropical Paradise? *Below*

The pink flamingoes in the Faught Garden harmonize beautifully with this island bed of white pansies and Greenland tulips.

Down to Earth *Page 238*

This antique rooster weathervane, with its distressed patina, has found a congenial new home at Plymouth, California's, Amador Flower Farm.

A Naturalistic Accent *Page 239*

Prairie dogs and cactus figures are highlighted by slender green leaves and a drift of yellow flowers.

Long-term Parking *Below*

Dick Cooper's rusty old flatbed truck becomes an eye-catching asset to the landscape when wreathed in verbena and hollyhocks.

Retirement Home *Above*
Two venerable farm implements salvaged from a scrap-yard have been put out to pasture in a field of Indian Blanket flowers near Austin, Texas.

Roadworthy *Overleaf*
Imagination has transformed an antique horsedrawn road scraper into a delightful raised tulip bed at this Volcano Road ranch in Amador County, California.

An Autumn Montage *Opposite*

This nostalgic grouping includes a red well pump, hand-crafted barrel, and old watering can highlighted by a pumpkin, chrysanthemums, and golden leaves, as photographed by the wayside in Bureau County, Illinois.

A Bountiful Barrow *Below*

The rusty old wheelbarrow below takes on new life with its colorful array of daffodils and pansies bursting from the soil. The barrow can be replanted with summer annuals after the danger of frost has passed.

In the Round *Opposite*

This creative composition was made with old telephone-cable spools in various sizes and other found objects of wood that appear to have taken root among the surrounding foliage and flowers.

Still Life with Daffodils *Below*

The free-form timber sculpture rises in graceful curves to frame spring's golden trumpets.

Prairie Country *Page 248*

An old wagon wheel and a rough-hewn fence softened by feathery grasses are central to this fall scene from the nation's heartland, captured on a road less traveled.

Glad Hands *Opposite*

A delightfully unexpected display of multicolored waving hands adds a humorous note between borders of vibrant summer flowers.

Fashioned with Care *Page 249*

A charming hand-crafted heart-shaped bentwood trellis presides over a bountiful flower bed at the Gandy Post Office in Logan County, Nebraska.

An Eye-catching Accent *Below*

Folk-art wooden tulips in a hanging bowl brighten the scene and allow unseasonal enjoyment of this colorful herald of spring.

Saluting the Flag

The spirit of independence reigns over the playful tributes to patriotism at right and below. Bold painting, found objects, and ingenuity add up to a spontaneous Fourth of July celebration.

❧ Index

Bibliography

Binetti, Marianne. *Shortcuts for Accenting Your Garden,* A Garden Way Publishing Book; Pownal, Vt.: Storey Communications, 1993.

Cox, Jeff, and Jerry Pavia. *Decorating Your Garden.* N.Y.: Abbeville Press, 1999.

Hill, May Brawley. *Furnishing the Old-Fashioned Garden.* N.Y.: Harry N. Abrams, 1998.

Lawrence, Elizabeth, ed. *The Gardener's Essential Gertrude Jekyll.* Boston: David R. Godine, 1986.

Lyons, Charlotte, with Mary Engelbreit and Barbara E. Martin. *Mary Engelbreit's Outdoor Companion.* Kansas City, Mo.: Andrews and McMeel, 1996.

Marchetti, Lauro, and Claire de Virieu, trans. Esme Howard. *Ninfa: A Roman Enchantment,* Small Books of Great Gardens series. N.Y.: Vendome Press, 1999.

Marinelli, Janet. "The Audubon Garden Makeover," *Audubon,* July/Aug 2000.

Morris, Alistair. *Antiques from the Garden.* Woodbridge, Eng.: Garden Art Press div., Antique Collectors' Club Ltd., 1996.

Smith, Linda Joan. *Smith & Hawken Garden Ornament.* N.Y.: Workman Publishing, 1998.

Stewart, Doug. "Fountains: Splash & Spectacle," *Smithsonian,* May 1998.

Strong, Roy. *Successful Small Gardens: New Designs for Time-Conscious Gardeners.* N.Y.: Rizzoli Intn'l., 1995.

Verey, Rosemary. *The Garden Gate,* Library of Garden Detail series. N.Y.: Simon & Schuster, 1992.

Weishan, Michael. *The New Traditional Garden: A Practical Guide to Creating and Restoring American Gardens for Homes of All Ages.* N.Y.: Ballantine Group, 1999.

Whitner, Jan K. *Stonescaping: A Guide to Using Stone in Your Garden,* A Garden Way Publishing Book; Pownal, Vt.: Storey Communications, 1995.

Williams, Bunny, with Nancy Drew. *On Garden Style.* N.Y.: Simon & Schuster, 1998.

Wolf, Rex. *Landscaping for Privacy: Hedges, Fences, Arbors,* Sunset Books; Menlo Park, Calif.: Lane Publishing, 1985.

Winterrowd, Wayne. "Planting Among the Stones: A Guide to Building and Embellishing a Terrace," *Horticulture,* Feb 1992.

Acknowledgments and Photo Credits

The publisher would like to thank the following individuals for their help in the preparation of this book: Sara Hunt, editor; Erin Pikor, photo editor; Charles J. Ziga, art director; Nikki L. Fesak, graphic designer; Lisa Langone Desautels, indexer. Grateful acknowledgment is also made to the owners of all the gardens illustrated in these pages and to the following individuals and institutions for permission to reproduce illustrations and photographs on the pages listed:

© **Mary Liz Austin:** 6,142-43, 82, 106, 244, 186; © **Barrett & MacKay: 2,** 26, 43, 61, 69, 75, 181, 182, 183, 184, 185; © **Ed Cooper:** 32-33, 54, 56-57, 73, 78, 84-85, 198-99, 110-11, 211, 214-15, 231, 232-33; © **Grace Davies:** 229; © **Terry Donnelly:** 44-45, 65, 66, 80, 86, 89, 92, 98-9, 104, 105, 108-09, 109,136-37, 188-89, 248; © **Nikki L. Fesak:** 12, 24, 25; © **Carolyn Fox:** 4, 17, 21, 28, 29, 30, 34-35, 36, 39, 42-43, 48, 49, 55, 58, 59, 62-63, 76, 126, 130, 132, 135, 145, 154, 160, 164, 164-65, 187, 193, 196, 197, 202-03, 206, 208-09, 216, 220, 224, 225, 227, 230, 233, 234-35, 236-37, 237, 238, 239, 240, 240-41, 242-43, 245, 249, 251; © **Blake Gardner: 46;** © **Rudi Holnsteiner:** 18, 37, 52, 53, 72, 103, 114, 114-15, 118, 121, 124-25,128, 129, 134, 140, 141, 149, 152, 153, 158, 159, 174, 191, 192, 194-95, 204, 204-05, 207, 210; © **Wolfgang Kaehler:** 32, 44, 60, 67, 90, 93, 96, 101,102-03, 107, 123, 131, 137, 138, 144, 150, 151, 155, 156-57, 167, 171, 172, 173, 175, 201, 226, 228; © **Balthazar Korab:** 11, 14, 50, 51, 179, 190, 218, 219, 212, 213, 221, 222, 223, 246, 247, 250, 252, 252-53; © **Paul Rocheleau:** 15, 16, 19, 27, 40-41, 64, 70-71, 74, 79, 81, 83, 86-7, 91, 94, 95,100,112, 116, 117, 119, 120, 122, 146, 147, 148, 162-63, 166, 170, 176; © **John Sylvester:** 13, 20, 31, 38, 88, 96-7, 113,161, 168; © **Charles J. Ziga:** 1, 3, 22, 23, 68, 133, 139, 169, 200. Hand-colored illustrations © **James P. Rodey III:** 8, 9, 10, 178, 180.